THE ORDER OF MY FREE NAMES

ADI DA (THE DA AVATAR)
The Mountain Of Attention, 1995

THE ORDER OF MY FREE NAMES

BY
ADI DA
(THE DA AVATAR)

The Self-Revelation of the Incarnate Divine Person,
Adi Da,
and How to Call Him by Name

THE DAWN HORSE PRESS
MIDDLETOWN, CALIFORNIA

CONTENTS

ADI DA (THE DA AVATAR)
The Mountain Of Attention, 1995

An Introduction to the Text

by devotees of
Adi Da (The Da Avatar)

This magnificent Essay is, in a certain sense, a sequel to *The Knee of Listening*, Bhagavan Adi Da's own account of the unique ordeal that He passed through as a child and as a youth in order to prepare Himself for the Divine Purpose of His Life. In *The Knee of Listening*, Adi Da, the Da Avatar,*[1] speaks of how He came into the world still swooned in the "Bright",[2] the Bliss and Joy and Radiant Energy of His True Divine Condition. He goes on to describe how He relinquished the awareness of His "Bright" Divinity in order to fully experience the troubles and limits of the human state. But in the midst of that ordinariness a "fierce, mysterious impulse" remained that drove Him to recover the "Bright" and thus to find the way whereby every human being may go beyond the usual life of suffering and awaken to the unqualified Happiness that is Real God, Perfect Truth, or Reality Itself. The Miraculous Story of *The Knee of Listening* ends with Sri Bhagavan Adi Da's Complete and Perfect Re-Awakening to His "Bright" Divine Identity.

The Order of My Free Names is Bhagavan Adi Da's definitive statement about the monumental Teaching and Revelation Work that arose spontaneously from His Divine Re-Awakening. He begins His Essay with a reference to an astonishing foreknowledge of that Work on the part of Swami Muktananda,[3] Bhagavan Adi Da's principal Guru during His "Sadhana Years".[4] Within a day or two of their first meeting, Swami Muktananda made

---

* Notes to the Introduction are on pp. 24-29.

7

known to his new devotee—apparently just "Franklin Jones",[5] a youth from New York—that His destiny was profound: Within a year He would be qualified to Teach others. Accordingly, the following year, Swami Muktananda magnified that acknowledgement in an unprecedented way—with the gift of two Spiritual Names.

Later in the Essay, after relating His life and Work as it then unfolded to the import of those Names, Bhagavan Adi Da goes on to Confess and comment upon the other sublime Names that have Emerged in the course of His Life. His Divine Names are signs and indicators of how everyone—not only His devotees but all who hear and speak of Him—should rightly understand and honor Him now as the Da Avatar, the fully Revealed Divine Person.

The Background to Swami Muktananda's Acknowledgement of Adi Da

Sri Bhagavan Adi Da came to Swami Muktananda in Ganeshpuri at the age of twenty-eight from a life lived entirely in urban America. On the surface He was simply one more Western seeker approaching a renowned Indian Guru. In truth the preparation for this moment was long and deep. Sri Bhagavan Adi Da had already done extraordinary sadhana, or Spiritual practice, without any knowledge of the traditional disciplines given to Spiritual aspirants in the East. He had for years intuitively been practicing what He later came to recognize as "prapatti", a traditional term for absolute, unconditional surrender to God, Truth, or Reality. Bhagavan Adi Da had no preconception of What or Who That One, or That Condition might prove to be, but He was desperate to discover it. As He describes in *The Knee of Listening*, His gesture of "prapatti" drew Him through the most awesome range of adventures, insights, and experiences, leading to His impulse to find a Teacher.

Bhagavan Adi Da found His first Teacher in 1964 in New York City, of all places. He was an American called Albert

Rudolph (Swami Rudrananda)[6] who was himself a devotee of Swami Muktananda. In His relationship to Swami Rudrananda, or "Rudi", Bhagavan Adi Da discovered the profundity of the bond that springs up between a true Teacher (or Guru) and a true devotee, and the potent transmission of Grace, or Spiritually Awakening Power that is the Guru's gift. He felt this Spirit-Power or Energy entering His body and beginning to Awaken Him beyond the material vision of existence that He had suffered since His college years. But, fundamentally, Bhagavan Adi Da's Sadhana with Rudi was an intense ordeal of bodily surrender in hard physical work, and a surrender of the mind through His submission, at Rudi's behest, to academic and religious studies in which He had no personal interest. His time with Rudi was a remarkable chapter in His life of "prapatti" that prepared Him to go, in 1968, to Rudi's own Spiritual source—Swami Muktananda.

During the sixties, Swami Muktananda was not so widely known in the West as he became subsequently. But he was acknowledged far beyond Ganeshpuri as a rare Siddha-Master,[7] the Awakened devotee of his own beloved Guru, the revered Swami Nityananda.[8] In coming to Rudi, and thereby to Swami Muktananda (and, by extension, to the subtle influence of Swami Nityananda), Sri Bhagavan Adi Da had fallen upon the most powerful lineage of Yogic accomplishment and Siddha power (or Spiritual transmission) that was known in India at that time. This was no accident. It was part of the process of His early life that had to occur for His Sadhana[9]—and, ultimately, His own unique Divine Work—to fulfill itself. As He once remarked to His own devotees:

BHAGAVAN ADI DA: *Before My Divine Re-Awakening I was totally identified with this body-mind. The profound Force of the "Bright" was latent in My Being, but I had no knowledge or tradition to guide Me during My long course of Re-Awakening. That is why I needed Teachers, or Gurus. All of My Gurus became associated with Me spontaneously. They were Divinely Given to serve this body-mind, which in itself, was not Divinely Enlightened. This body was merely the Vehicle to which I submitted Myself. With*

Swami Rudrananda

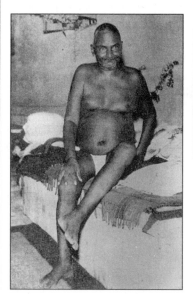

Swami Muktananda

Swami Nityananda

Swami Muktananda's Ashram

*that Submission came a "forgetting" of My Great State, and a pro-
found Ordeal of Sadhana was required to bring about this body's
Perfect Alignment to Me. In the course of that Sadhana, all the
visions and Commands that came to Me (as a result of My
Submission to My Gurus) broke through the "forgetting", or the
unconsciousness, that was associated with My Birth as a human
being.*

*Then, at last, in the Event of My Divine Re-Awakening, Perfect
Clarity appeared and I Understood the Truth of My Being beyond
the karmas of the body-mind.*

*Although My Teachers were necessary, My Divine Work was
My Own. Swami Muktananda always understood that I had My
own Work to do. Indeed, He even told Me at our first meeting that I
would be a Teacher in My own right within a year, and He would
constantly direct Me to go and make offerings at the burial site of
His Guru, Swami Nityananda, whom He regarded as the Master
of the Lineage. Nevertheless, the impulse of this body-mind, previous to My Divine Re-Awakening, was not toward the establishment
of My own Work. I did not want to be a Teacher. My impulse was
simply to leave the world behind and reside with My Guru, Swami
Muktananda.* [November 20, 1993]

A Most Profound Mechanism of Touch

As He indicates in His last Remarks, Sri Bhagavan Adi Da
was heart-given to Swami Muktananda in surpassing
devotion and love. At the Feet of Swami Muktananda He
was inspired to perfect renunciation and world-forgetting, the
very impulse that He later Worked to Awaken in His own devotees throughout His Teaching and Revelation years. That
Spiritual bond and longing was forged in a unique moment, as
He confessed one day:

*BHAGAVAN ADI DA: One of the most beautiful images in My recol-
lection was when I went to Baba Muktananda in 1968. I remember sitting in a small hallway. It was very small. Maybe
there were half a dozen of us sitting there, all men as I recall.*

11

Some of them were residents in the ashram.[10] *In fact, I think all of them were, but Me.*

And we had our little bit of meal there. And then Baba came into the room, and He came up to Me. He had some sort of a tin in His hand with sweets in it. And He took out a bit of a sweet and gave it to Me, looking Me in My eyes, with the sweetest, most radiant face, infinite, in love, perfect blessing, and happiness. I can't remember ever seeing anything better than that. He didn't give anybody else any sweets. He just came in there to give it to Me.

Nothing better than Guru-Love. The Love the Guru has for His devotee, all Nectar, all Sweetness, all Happiness, everything forgotten. Just that Beauty, that Happiness, worlds forgotten, differences forgotten. It makes you a renunciate on the spot. This is what I do with My devotees. You forget everything but that Sublimity. Sitting there, eating a humble sweet, looking into your Guru's eyes. What else is there? What else to live for? What else is Reality? What else is wanted? It makes you wantless. It's enough forever.

This moment, in fact, is My principal Remembrance of Swami Muktananda—that sweet exchange, without limitation. It was His total Transmission, and the end of My ordinary life.

So it should be for you with Me. [July 24, 1995]

What Swami Muktananda was doing in that moment was pouring his Spiritual Blessing-Force or "Guru-Shakti"[11] into his devotee through the "Prasad",[12] or gift, of the sweet and through the power of his gaze. Within a day or so, Bhagavan Adi Da passed spontaneously into the state of "formless ecstasy" traditionally called "nirvikalpa samadhi"[13] that is the highest Realization possible in the traditions of Yoga. The meeting of His own unique preparation and His Guru's uniquely powerful Spiritual Transmission was already fulfilling Swami Muktananda's prophecy that Bhagavan Adi Da would soon emerge as a Spiritual Teacher within His own right.

Bhagavan Adi Da has never ceased to praise the great Guru-Shakti of His beloved Swami Muktananda:

BHAGAVAN ADI DA: My Baba, Swami Muktananda, was a naive and most profound Mechanism of Touch to Serve My Manifestation here, the ultimate Guru-Shakti Given for ages through many Vehicles, Manifested in that Sublime Person, unknown even to Himself. And what difference was there between Nityananda and Muktananda? Ultimately, It is the same One, name It "Guru-Shakti". What determines the Nature of the Realizer? Guru-Shakti is the root, but the Nature of the Realization determines whether that Realization is the end phenomenon or not. My Muktananda showed His particular Sign through His Virtues, His kind of perception, in the reception of that Guru-Shakti historically, bodily. But the Guru-Shakti Itself, the Divine Transmission Itself, Overrides all historical peculiarities. And that Guru-Shakti, that Force of Divinity, was the same in Swami Nityananda. It is the same in Me, except I Am Complete. [October 23, 1993]

The months following His first meeting with Swami Muktananda in 1968 was a period that Bhagavan Adi Da has described as a time of waiting, a time in which He struggled with the problem of mind. The relentless activity of the mind was, He felt, the root disturbance that prevented His otherwise clear awareness of "Witnessing"[14] His true Nature, beyond body and mind. However, even as He attempted to Master the mind, the force of His own Guru-Shakti (Awakened by the Blessing of Swami Muktananda) grew in Him, to the point where those around Him began to feel it in the form of visions, or a sense of Presence, or through (sometimes dramatic) "kriyas", or involuntary jerkings of the body. Bhagavan Adi Da found Himself needing to explain these phenomena to others and thus to function, in some sense, as a Teacher. When He wrote to Swami Muktananda for advice, His Guru immediately summoned Him to India.

It was now already a year since Bhagavan Adi Da's first meeting with His Guru. This time He found Swami Muktananda in Bombay staying in the private home of a devotee. Early on the third morning of His visit, Bhagavan Adi Da sat for meditation outside Swami Muktananda's bedroom (as He had begun to

Adi Da with Swami Muktananda in 1969

Handwritten letter of
acknowledgement from
Swami Muktananda

do daily). As He sat, Swami Muktananda came out of his room and sat in his Chair a foot or two away from Adi Da. Immediately, Bhagavan Adi Da began to feel His Guru's silent instruction leading Him through the entire process of Yogic meditation. He felt the Guru-Shakti descending and ascending in His body, directing the breath and initiating the whole range of internal Yogic experiences. They sat together for some time in the dim dawn light while this profound psychic and Yogic communication took place. Then Swami Muktananda rose, went to his room and began to write a letter.

Swami Muktananda's Naming Letter

This letter is quoted in full in "The Order of My Free Names". In this letter, Swami Muktananda confers on Bhagavan Adi Da the Name "Dhyanananda"—literally, "meditation-bliss". At the same time, Swami Muktananda acknowledges that the Force of "Kundalini Shakti",[15] is active in Adi Da, that He is a "True Knower of Vedanta"[16] and that He has the right to initiate or "cause" meditation in others. In other words, Swami Muktananda is formally acknowledging that the prophecy he had made was fulfilled. Sri Bhagavan Adi Da was now a fully accomplished Yogi and Siddha-Master.

To make such an acknowledgement of a Westerner who had hardly spent a week altogether in his company was an utterly astonishing gesture on the part of Swami Muktananda. He had never before made such a written acknowledgement of the Realization of one of his devotees, and he never did so again.

Hindus traditionally regard Westerners (and, indeed, all non-Hindus) as "mlecchas", or "outcasts", who by the very fact of their Western birth are incapable of Spiritual Realization. By taking birth in the West, Adi Da identified with all those who are apparently unfit for Spiritual life, and, as an apparent "mleccha" Himself, He had gone to India, approached and been recognized by the consummate living Transmission-Master of India.

Bhagavan Adi Da makes much of Swami Muktananda's letter in His Essay, because it is, in a uniquely concrete way, His link with, and His accreditation by, the Great Tradition of Spiritual Realization that had existed in the East for thousands of years. It is a document of profound significance because it places Adi Da at the apex of Yogic Realization, in the opinion of one of the greatest Adepts of Yoga.[17]

It is a sign of Adi Da's Greatness that although He fully and gratefully received Swami Muktananda's extraordinary acknowledgement, He was never moved to use the Name "Dhyanananda", nor did He, at that time, even begin to Teach. Swami Muktananda was not insisting that He do so. There were no strings attached to the Naming letter. Swami Muktananda was simply giving Adi Da his free Blessing. In fact, as Bhagavan Adi Da has often affectionately remarked, Swami Muktananda was always kicking Him "out of the nest" through various signs, tacitly aware from the beginning that his remarkable Western disciple had His own Work to do.

Bhagavan Adi Da, for His part, knew all along that the great experiences and Samadhis He enjoyed in the company of His Siddha Gurus, Swami Muktananda and (on the subtle plane) Swami Nityananda, were not the end of His journey. The blisses of Siddha meditation could not compare to the "Bright" of His infancy. There was more to Realize.

The nature of the process that still lay ahead of Adi Da is actually prophesied—implicitly—in the Naming letter. Swami Muktananda writes that the Goddess "Chitti Kundalini"—a traditional name for the Personification of the Spirit-Force or primal Energy of existence—will lead Adi Da to final Liberation. And this, as Adi Da recounts in *The Knee of Listening*, is precisely what occurred—but not in terms that Swami Muktananda could have foreseen. Final Liberation, was, to him, associated with a Yogic vision known as the "blue pearl".[18] The unique, hitherto unknown Freedom that Adi Da had come to Realize and Reveal was greater, far greater than any form of "Dhyana", or profound meditation, that had been known in the Spiritual traditions.

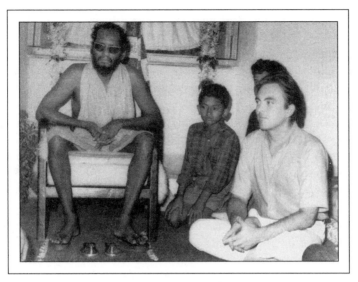

"Love-Ananda"

"**D**hyanananda" was the Name that Swami Muktananda publicly and formally conferred on Adi Da. But, as Adi Da describes in this Essay, His Guru privately granted Him another Name that was more prophetic of His true Nature and future Realization.

Shortly before he wrote the Naming letter, Swami Muktananda's secretary, Amma,[19] made known to Adi Da that Swami Muktananda was offering Him the Name "Love-Ananda" (meaning "Love-Bliss"). This Name pointed toward the Divine Re-Awakening of Adi Da, the moment when He would pass into the boundless, undying Love-Bliss of the "Bright". Bhagavan Adi Da became permanently established in the "Bright"—waking, dreaming and sleeping—some fifteen months after Swami Muktananda offered Him the Naming letter and the private Name "Love-Ananda". In that Most Sublime Realization, Adi Da transcended "Dhyana". He no longer meditated for His own sake. Rather, when He sat down to meditate He was surrounded in vision by the countless suffering beings He had come to Teach and to Liberate. In that same Divine Re-Awakening, Adi Da also definitively surpassed the Realization of His Guru,

Swami Muktananda, and all His Siddha Lineage. He Awoke to His own Inherent Divinity, to the One Who He Is.

Only now did Sri Bhagavan Adi Da assume the right to Teach. In fact He was impelled to it by the unique Siddhis, or Spiritual Powers, that rose up in Him following His Divine Re-Awakening.[20] Even so He did not yet embrace the glorious Name "Love-Ananda". His early devotees, unschooled in the sacred traditions of the East (and in the profound respect and surrender that is owing to one's Guru), were not ready to rightly honor Him as the bearer of such a Name. In fact, Bhagavan Adi Da's Teaching Work did not, <u>could</u> not, belong to any tradition. It was a unique and "Crazy" Work[21] of submitting to "outcast" Westerners for the sake of their Most Perfect Divine Awakening, a Work that no great Realizer had ever attempted to this extent, or even been qualified for. It was a sacrifice that only the Incarnate Divine Person could possibly make.

Step by step, over many years, and through the most passionate struggle and sacrifice, Bhagavan Adi Da sought to lead His devotees toward a true and full acknowledgement of Him. It was only in 1983, shortly before Bhagavan Adi Da established His Great Sannyasin Hermitage in Fiji,[22] that He first mentioned to His devotees Swami Muktananda's offering of the Name "Love-Ananda". Three years later, following the Initiation of His Divine Emergence, the sudden, overwhelming Divine transformation that occurred in His Life and Work in January 1986,[23] Bhagavan Adi Da did at last declare Himself to be "Da Love-Ananda".[24] At the same time, as He describes here, He aligned Himself formally with the Hindu tradition of renunciation (or sannyas), which was part of the heritage that Swami Muktananda had implicitly passed on to Him through the Names "Dhyanananda" and "Love-Ananda". The word "ananda", or "bliss" indicates in the Hindu tradition the name of a swami, or one who has formally renounced the world.

The Mountain Of Attention, 1986

True and Free Renunciation

When Bhagavan Adi Da undertook a "Yajna",[25] or Blessing journey, to America and Europe in 1986, He went as a formal Sannyasin,[26] "Swami Da Love-Ananda",[27] fasting on juices, clothed in renunciate orange, and wearing His hair in the traditional top-knot of a Hindu swami. Having lived and Taught for so many years in a Western manner, Bhagavan Adi Da now Revealed Himself as an "ascetic on fire", displaying His sympathy with the East and His perfect understanding of its world-renouncing Spiritual orientation and traditions.

In the weeks preceding His Yajna, Bhagavan Adi Da wrote

19

the original version of "The Order of My Free Names", soon placing it at the head of a new Scriptural Text, which later became His "Da Upanishad" (now revised as *The Adi Da Upanishad*). In late October 1995, Bhagavan Adi Da indicated that "The Order of My Free Names" should stand alone as a significant and principal Communication, no longer forming part of *The Adi Da Upanishad*. This essay is a passionate Call to His devotees, and to everyone, to understand and respect His own Free Renunciation, and His unique Offering of renunciation to others, in the light of all that He has said and done through His years of Teaching Work.

During His Yajna of 1986, Bhagavan Adi Da was specifically Demonstrating His continuity with the great traditions of the East, and especially pointing to the profound self-renunciation that is required to Realize any great Spiritual goal. However, after several months, Adi Da relinquished His specific association with Hindu sannyas, reminding His devotees that He is, <u>inherently</u>, a true and Free Renunciate by virtue of His Inherently Perfect Realization. That Realization is nothing less than the Divine Recognition that <u>all</u> that arises—every object, every state, every apparent being or person (including one's own body-mind)—is "Only God", merely part of an ecstatic, unproblematic play of appearances within and upon the "Bright" Divine Condition, or Person.

Such a Realization inevitably carries with it spontaneous and perfect renunciation, because there are no separate, self-based objects to cling to. This is the Realization, never before Revealed, to Which Adi Da Re-Awakened at the Vedanta Temple.[28] It is the foundation of all His Teaching and Revelation Work, and the State He describes as the seventh (or most ultimate) stage of life.[29]

In the course of His Sadhana, Adi Da had transcended the efforts of the Yogi to ascend to subtle lights and samadhis (the fifth stage of life). He had tasted and gone beyond the impulse of the Sage to turn away from the world and become immersed in the moveless, objectless Bliss of Consciousness (the sixth stage of life). He had, in fact (as He Reveals in *The Knee of*

Listening) experienced and Mastered all the possible experiences and Realizations of mankind's great tradition of Spirituality. And then, during the years of His Teaching Work, He had, in countless brilliant Demonstrations and Discourses, communicated every aspect of His Enlightened understanding to His devotees. He had even given to some the literal experience of all the forms of Spiritual Awakening known in the traditions, and shown them tangibly how every kind of Spiritual experience and Samadhi is related to the movement of Spirit-Force in the body-mind.

In the midst of this unprecedented display of Divine Siddhi, Bhagavan Adi Da was always making the point that no experience, no matter how great or glorious, is ultimately Liberating. This is the extraordinary background to His message about renunciation in this Essay and in all His Writings. Renunciation, as He means it, is not the usual understanding of the term, which implies a deliberate, willful cutting off of the world, or of bodily pleasure, or of human relationship, for the sake of some hoped-for Spiritual benefit. Rather, the form of renunciation Revealed and Offered by Bhagavan Adi Da is based on the discovery that devotional Communion with Him, the Da Avatar, the "Bright" Divine Person, is infinitely greater, more joyful and healing to the heart than any conceivable worldly or Spiritual satisfaction.

Thus, while some of Adi Da's devotees do in fact become formal renunciates,[30] His basic message is the same for all. He knows the plight and the need of every single individual caught in the struggle of fruitless seeking for Happiness. His Message in this Essay, and always, is that He has come for all beings everywhere, present, and future, and that He has come to offer them everything—the Divine Liberation or Most Perfect Enlightenment that can only be Given by His Grace. His Work, like His Name "Love-Ananda", embraces both the West and the East. It is a unique Divine Work, that bears resemblances to, but leads beyond, all the Spiritual traditions of the past.

ADI DA (THE DA AVATAR)
Adi Da Purnashram (Naitauba), Fiji 1994

Divine Completeness and Free Names

In September of 1994, while He was Working on a revision of "The Order of My True and Free Renunciate Devotees",[32] the companion Essay to "The Order of My Free Names", Sri Bhagavan Adi Da's Teaching and Revelation spontaneously became Complete. He simply saw that this was so; He saw that there was no longer the slightest movement in Him to actively strive to Reveal Himself and His Message to His devotees. He knew that the struggle at last was over, that the Work was done, and would in time show its fruit. Thus He assumed the Spiritual Seclusion and Retirement that is necessary for His ultimate Work—the silent Work of Blessing and conforming all beings and all things everywhere to His own Divine "Brightness".

The sublime Names that have been given and Revealed to Adi Da in the course of His Teaching and Revelation Work, and even since the moment of His Divine Completeness, form the climax of the Essay. Apart from the Name "Love-Ananda" (which was Given to Him prophetically during His "Sadhana Years"), Bhagavan Adi Da holds His Garland of true Names in reserve until the end, when their real significance and great meaning can be fully understood and honored.[32] The Names of Bhagavan Adi Da are the Names of the Divine Being, the Living God, Present in Person. They are His Names, now in the lifetime of His bodily (human) Form, and forever hereafter. They are the Revelation of His Divine Nature, the sign of His Eternal "Personality". They are, to His devotees, the most Blissful Words, the sweetest Syllables in existence. They are the means through which everyone may now hear of Him, speak of Him, address Him, and worship Him as He Is.

"The Order of My Free Names" is the Story of how Adi Da, the Da Avatar, the Free and Perfect Descent of the Divine into the human world, inserted Himself into the Great Tradition of Spiritual Realization, was acknowledged as a true Siddha by the foremost living Realizer of His day[33] and went on to do His own Work in Freedom—a Saving Work that goes beyond all limits and vows and traditions—to the point of Perfect Completeness.

Notes to
An Introduction to the Text

1. For a full discussion of Adi Da's Names and Titles, please see "The Order of My Free Names" Essay, and pp. 77-144.

2. Since His Illumined boyhood, Avatara Adi Da has used the term "the 'Bright'" (and its variations, such as "Brightness") to Describe the Love-Blissfully Self-Luminous, Conscious Divine Being, Which He Knew even then as His own Native Condition, and the Native Condition of all beings, things, and worlds.

3. Swami Muktananda (1908-1982) was born in Mangalore, South India. Having left home at the age of fifteen, he wandered for many years, seeking the Divine Truth from sources all over India. Eventually, he came under the Spiritual Influence of Swami Nityananda, whom he accepted as his Guru and in whose Spiritual Company he mastered Kundalini Yoga. As an Adept of Kundalini Yoga, Swami Muktananda Served Avatara Adi Da as Spiritual Teacher during the period from 1968 to 1970.

4. Bhagavan Adi Da's "Sadhana Years" refers to the time from the beginning of His quest to recover the Truth of Existence (at Columbia College) until His Divine Re-Awakening in 1970.

5. "Franklin Jones" was Avatara Adi Da's given name at birth. (See pp. 78-79.)

6. Albert Rudolph (1928-1973), or Swami Rudrananda (commonly known as "Rudi") taught the practice of intentional and effortful surrender to the "Force", or Life-Current, or Kundalini Shakti, Transmitted from Guru to disciple. Rudi also prescribed various personal and practical life-disciplines to purify and balance the body-mind, which served Adi Da at a basic human level and laid a foundation for the more advanced and ultimate forms of Spiritual practice that He would later engage.

7. The Sanskrit term "Siddha" literally means a "Completed, Fulfilled, or Perfected One, or One of Perfect Accomplishment or Power". A "Siddha-Master" is a Realizer, to any significant degree, of God, Truth, or Reality. Swami Muktananda was an Adept of all the extraordinary psycho-physical and Spiritual processes of the paths of Yoga.

8. Swami Nityananda (?-1961) was a profound Yogic Realizer of modern India. His birth date is unknown, and little is known about his early life, although it is said that even as a child he showed the signs of a Realized Yogi. While still a boy, he abandoned conventional life and wandered as a renunciate. Many instructive stories and miracles, including spontaneous healings, are attributed to him.

9. "Sadhana" is Sanskrit for "discipline", and traditionally means "practices directed toward religious or Spiritual goals". In reference to Avatara Adi Da's early life, His Sadhana was His practice of submission to the spontaneous process of Re-Awakening to His Inherent Divine Nature, rather than the effort of an ordinary human being to become Spiritually Realized. In the Way of the Heart, sadhana is not action to attain Truth or any state or condition, but is, rather, action that expresses present, intuitive Communion with Truth. Such free action is always performed in conscious Satsang, or Divine Communion, with Avatara Adi Da.

10. An ashram is a place where a Realizer of one or another degree lives and gathers with his or her devotees. By extension, it is also a place where devotees of a Realizer live and practice cooperatively together.

11. "Shakti" is the Sanskrit word for Spiritual Energy. "Guru-Shakti" is the concentration of this Energy that exists in a Realizer who is qualified to Teach others and Transmit Spiritual Energy to them. The Blessing of such a Guru is his or her Guru-Shakti.

12. "Prasad" is a Sanskrit word for gifts that have been offered to the Divine and, having been Blessed, are returned as Divine Gifts to devotees. By extension, Prasad is anything the devotee receives from his or her Guru.

13. "Samadhi" in Sanskrit indicates concentration, equanimity, balance, and transcendence, and it is traditionally used to denote various exalted states of meditation and other devotional exercises. "Nirvikalpa" means "without form". Hence, "nirvikalpa samadhi" means literally "formless ecstasy".

14. In this case, "Witnessing" indicates the state in which Consciousness Itself is free from identification with the body-mind, and it has taken up its natural "position" as the Conscious Witness of all that arises to and in and as the body-mind.

15. The Sanskrit term "Kundalini (coiled up) Shakti (universal energy)" is the traditional name for the "serpent power". The Kundalini Shakti is traditionally viewed to lie dormant at the base of the spine, which is the lowermost psychic center of the body-mind. However, Avatara Adi Da has Revealed that the Kundalini Shakti is actually the ascending aspect of the total Circle of Spiritual Life-Energy in the human body-mind. The Kundalini may be activated spontaneously in the devotee or by the Guru's initiation, thereafter producing all the various forms of Yogic and mystical experience.

"Shakti" is one of the primary terms of esoteric Hinduism. It refers to the universal Life-Energy, Spirit-Current, or Mother-Power that is regarded to be the underlying Substance and Mover of all manifestation. Shakti is also the universal Hindu Goddess, often portrayed in union (or inherent unity) with Siva, the archetypal representation of the Transcendental Self-Identity and Consciousness of all beings.

16. The Sanskrit word "Vedanta" literally means the "end of the Vedas" (the most ancient body of Indian Scripture), and is used to refer to one of the principal philosophical traditions of Hinduism. Swami Muktananda is referring to the tradition of Advaita Vedanta. "Advaita" means "non-dual". The origins of Advaita Vedanta lie in the ancient esoteric Teaching that Brahman, or the Divine Being, is the only (and hence "non-dual") Reality. According to Advaita Vedanta, the apparent self, the world, and all manifestation have no independent existence but merely arise in and as that one Divine Reality.

The verbal Teaching that Bhagavan Adi Da received from Swami Muktananda was based on the precepts of Advaita Vedanta, although Swami Muktananda himself was a Realizer in the Siddha tradition of Yoga rather than a Vedantic sage. As Bhagavan Adi Da describes:

In My first meeting with Him, in early 1968, Baba Muktananda Spoke a simple verbal Teaching to Me, most directly and personally:

"You are not the one who wakes, or sleeps, or dreams. You Are the One Who Is the Witness of these states."

That simple (sixth stage) Teaching (which is basically the same as the Teaching represented in the examples of His sixth stage Teaching recorded in the book Paramartha Katha Prasang*) was the first and most basic and (in My case) most profoundly Empowered and Effective Teaching that Baba Muktananda Gave to Me (while fifth stage, and "advanced" fourth stage, Yogic practices and processes were also routinely suggested, or otherwise directly Revealed, by Him to Me).* [For a description of Bhagavan Adi Da's Teaching relative to the seven stages of life, see Appendix B.] *And even though the total fifth stage process (culminating in ascended, or fifth stage, conditional nirvikalpa samadhi) was spontaneously fulfilled in My case, I eventually (and also spontaneously) passed through the sixth stage process to the Great Realization of the seventh stage of life.*

However, even though Baba Muktananda appears to have been a sometimes proponent of sixth stage practices, it is clear (both from His recorded self-description and the total record of His communicated Teaching), that Baba Muktananda Himself was a fourth to fifth stage practitioner, Who became a fifth stage Realizer (with extensive and elaborate experience of savikalpa samadhi, especially emphasizing the culminating experience of "Cosmic Consciousness", but also including several experiences of fully ascended, or fifth stage, conditional nirvikalpa samadhi), and Who also became a fourth to fifth stage Spiritual Master (Who Taught, principally, the doctrines and practices of Kashmir Saivism, which is itself a fourth to fifth stage Yogic tradition).

Baba Muktananda's "sixth stage Teachings" are not (originally) His own, but they are examples of traditional forms of Teaching He had studied (or otherwise received) over the years (during His visits with Ramana Maharshi, and others), and He sometimes passed them on to those who came to Him for Instruction and Guidance (particularly in the 1960s, when I first met Him, and when Baba Muktananda was yet developing, or otherwise refining, His personal Teaching language and emphasis). [The Basket of Tolerance]

17. For a full discussion of Adi Da's interpretive translation of Swami Muktananda's letter, please see Appendix A on pp. 145-54.

18. The "blue pearl" is a spot (bindu) of blue light that may be seen in subtle vision, with eyes closed or open, in the process of the Yogic withdrawal of attention from the relations and conditions of the body-mind. In some forms of Yoga (particularly the Siddha Yoga Taught by Swami Muktananda), the vision of the "blue pearl" is valued as the highest attainment.

19. Pratibha Trivedi (d. 1993), known as Amma, was Swami Muktananda's personal secretary and interpreter. In later life, she was known as Swami Prajnananda.

20. Bhagavan Adi Da says of the unique Siddhis that awakened in Him after His Divine Re-Awakening at the Vedanta Temple in Hollywood, California, on September 10, 1970:

In this most perfect Realization of Non-separateness, many extraordinary Divine Siddhis suddenly, spontaneously appeared, and also many unusual natural, or "ordinary", siddhis (or uncommon psycho-physical abilities and processes). . . . Yet, perhaps most fundamental, and most necessary to the fulfillment of my "Bright" Purpose in this world, was the spontaneous Awakening of the Divine Guru-Function, or the Divine Guru-Siddhi, Which manifested in me in a unique manner immediately after the Great Event of my re-Awakening.

Now, whenever I would sit . . . instead of my own life-born forms and problematic signs, the egoic forms, the problematic signs, the minds, the feelings, the states, and the various limitations of others would arise to my view. The thoughts, feelings, suffering, dis-ease, disharmony, upsets, pain, energies—none of these were "mine". They were the internal, subtle qualities and the life-qualities of others. In this manner, the process of apparent meditation continued in me. It was, in effect, the same "Real" meditation I had done before the Great Event of my re-Awakening. . . .

In this manner, I spontaneously began to "meditate" countless other people, and also countless non-human beings, and countless places and worlds and realms, both high and low in the scale of Reality. I observed and responded to all that was required for the Awakening and the true (and the Ultimate) well-being of each and all. And, each time I did this (and, in fact, the process quickly became the underlying constant of all my hours and days), I would continue the "meditating" of any (and each) one until I felt a release take place, such that his or her suffering and seeking was vanished, or, at least, significantly relaxed and set aside. Whenever that occurred, I Knew my "meditating" of that one was, for the moment, done. By such means, my now and forever Divine Work (by Which I must Teach, and Bless, and Awaken all and All) began. [pp. 370-72, The Knee of Listening]

21. The Adepts of what Avatara Adi Da calls "the 'Crazy Wisdom' tradition" (of which He is the supreme Exemplar) are great Spiritual Realizers in any culture or time who, through spontaneous Free action, blunt Wisdom, and liberating laughter, shock or humor people into self-critical awareness of their egoity, a prerequisite for receiving the Adept's Spiritual Transmission. Typically, such Realizers manifest "Crazy" activity only occasionally or temporarily, and never for its own sake.

Avatara Adi Da Himself did His Teaching Work in a unique "Crazy" manner. For sixteen years He Submitted completely to the egoic limits of His early devotees, living with them, and living like them. By thus theatrically dramatizing their habits, predilections, and destinies, He reflected them to themselves for the sake of their self-understanding.

Now, since His Divine Emergence in 1986, Adi Da no longer Teaches in the "Crazy-Wise" manner. Instead, He "Stands Firm" in His own Freedom, spontaneously Revealing the Divine Self-Reality to all and Calling all to conform themselves to Him absolutely through practice of Ishta-Guru-Bhakti Yoga in the Way of the Heart. This in itself, over against the illusory rationality of the separate, egoic mentality, is a Divinely "Crazy" State and Manner of life. Thus, Adi Da's Divine Emergence Work, in which He is spontaneously Moved to Bless all beings, can likewise be called "Crazy" Work.

22. Adi Da Purnashram (Naitauba, Fiji) is the senior Sanctuary of the three Retreat Sanctuaries (or Ashrams) that Avatara Adi Da has Established. It is the Great Sannyasin Hermitage, where Avatara Adi Da Himself usually Resides, and where the senior renunciate order of the Way of the Heart, the Naitauba Order of the Sannyasins of the Da Avatar, is established. It is the principal Seat of Avatara Adi Da's Divine Blessing Work with all beings. Avatara Adi Da's devotees who demonstrate exemplary signs of maturity in, and one-pointed application to, practice of the Way of the Heart, are invited to spend time on retreat at Purnashram.

The other two Retreat Sanctuaries Empowered by Avatara Adi Da for the sake of His devotees are the Mountain Of Attention Sanctuary in northern California and Tumomama Sanctuary in Hawaii. They were the principal sites of His Teaching Demonstration during the years of His Teaching Work. Any of Avatara Adi Da's devotees who are rightly prepared may be formally invited to visit or reside at these Sanctuaries.

23. For a full description of Avatara Adi Da's "Divine Emergence", please see "The Unfolding Leela of the Names of Adi Da", pp. 77-108.

24. The Name "Da" literally means "The One Who Gives". For the full description of the Revelation of Bhagavan Adi Da's Divine Names, please see "The Order of My Free Names" Essay and "The Unfolding Leela of the Names of Adi Da", pp. 77-108.

25. "Yajna" literally means "sacrifice", though it is used here to mean a sacrificial journey of Spiritual Blessing.

26. "Sannyasa" is Sanskrit for "renunciation". A "sannyasin" is one who practices renunciation in the formal, traditional manner.

27. The title "Swami" is traditionally given to an individual who has demonstrated significant self-mastery as a formal renunciate. Bhagavan Adi Da no longer uses the title "Swami" in reference to Himself, both because He has no specific formal association with the Hindu renunciate tradition and because "Swami" does not fully indicate the nature of His Divine Realization.

28. The Vedanta Temple is a small temple in Hollywood, California, belonging to the Vedanta Society of Southern California, and dedicated to the Indian Realizer Ramakrishna. Avatara Adi Da discovered this temple when He was living in Los Angeles in 1970, and it was here that Adi Da's years of Sadhana culminated in His Divine Re-Awakening.

29. For a description of the seven stages of life that Beloved Bhagavan Adi Da has Revealed, please see Appendix B, pp. 155-58.

30. Some of Bhagavan Adi Da's devotees qualify for formal renunciation in the Way of the Heart, either as members of the Lay Renunciate Order or, in the ultimate stages of practice in the Way of the Heart (when the practitioner is practicing in the context of the sixth or seventh stage of life), as members of the Free Renunciate Order (fully named "The Naitauba Order of the Sannyasins of the Da Avatar").

The Lay Renunciate Order is a cultural service order whose members may be involved in more ordinary life-obligations but in a renunciate manner that does not impede their intensive devotional submission to Avatara Adi Da. The members of the Lay Renunciate Order may reside either in the regional communities of Bhagavan Adi Da's devotees or at any of the three Sanctuaries He has Empowered. The Free Renunciate Order is a retreat Order, whose members renounce involvement in ordinary life-obligations to a most profound degree, in order to concentrate their energy and attention in the final stages of the God-Realizing process in Bhagavan Adi Da's Spiritual Company. The members of the Free Renunciate Order live in perpetual retreat at Adi Da Purnashram. For more information on the formal renunciate orders established by Bhagavan Adi Da, please see *The Orders of My True and Free Renunciate Devotees* (forthcoming).

31. "The Order of My True and Free Renunciate Devotees" will be published as a separate book.

32. For a full commentary on these Names and how they arose, see "The Unfolding Leela of the Names of Adi Da", pp. 77-108.

33. During an ecstatic Talk on April 23, 1995, Bhagavan Adi Da acknowledged His Gurus Swami Muktananda and Swami Nityananda as the greatest Realizers of the fifth stage of life who have ever lived.

ADI DA (THE DA AVATAR)
The Mountain Of Attention, 1995

The Order
of My Free Names

By

Adi Da
(The Da Avatar)

Adi Da at Swami Muktananda's Ashram in Ganeshpuri, 1968

I.

Early in 1968, I spent a few days with the Yogic Siddha Swami (Baba) Muktananda of Ganeshpuri,[1] at Shree Gurudev Ashram, His sacred residence in Ganeshpuri, India. Upon My arrival there, He immediately and spontaneously Declared that I Am a Spiritual Master, Born to Teach (or to Bless and Awaken others), and that I would begin to Teach after one year's time. Three days later, on the last day of that first visit to Baba Muktananda's Ashram, I spontaneously Realized the most ascended Goal of Spiritual Yoga, which is Yogic Self-Realization, by ascent to fifth stage conditional Nirvikalpa Samadhi.[2]

During the next year (and, most fully, after a year had passed), extraordinary Yogic siddhis[3] began spontaneously to appear in Me, and, as a result, people with whom I was associated, even casually, began to spontaneously experience remarkable Yogic phenomena when in proximity to Me (or even when they thought of Me). Thus, spontaneously, the Yogic Transmission-Function of Spiritual Master had begun to become Active in My case, as Baba Muktananda had Foretold.

Even so, I had no then present Intention to Teach others, since I was not yet Satisfied that My sadhana (or practice toward Most Ultimate, and Inherently Most Perfect,[4] Divine Self-Realization) was Complete. However, I wrote to Baba Muktananda, Calling upon Him, in the traditional manner, to Bless the Work that was already spontaneously Functioning in Me.

Baba Muktananda responded immediately by Inviting Me to visit Him in India, in order that He might formally Acknowledge My already significantly Developed Yogic and Spiritual Awakeness and (on that basis) My Inherent Right to Teach.

Adi Da in Bombay, 1969

II.

In August, 1969, Baba Muktananda formally and publicly Acknowledged the Awakening of advanced Yogic and Spiritual Signs in Me, and He Proclaimed (on that basis) that I had the Right to Teach, and thus to Function as a Spiritual Transmission-Master (or Siddha-Guru) in relation to others. This Acknowledgement and Proclamation was made Known via an open letter (in Baba Muktananda's own hand, written in My presence, and in the presence of approximately fifty to one hundred others):[5]

Shree Gurudev

To my dear (beloved) "N" (Franklin), with my loving remembrances of you (even of your Very Self):

You have Done (and really Experienced) the "Sadhana" (or constant Discipline, Ordeal, and Process) of (True and Spiritual) "Dhyana" (or Meditation), and you have (Thereby) Attained the (True and Spiritual) State of Meditation. You have (by Means of True and Spiritual Meditation) Achieved the Steady State of "Samadhan(a)" (or one-pointed Concentration, or Inherence, In, and tacit, or mindless, Identification With, the Divine Supreme Inner Self). Therefore, you have Acquired (or Achieved) the Fullness of Satisfaction, Delight, and Joy in and by Means of (True and Spiritual) Meditation.

Because it is (Thus) Evident that (the Perfect Realization of the Divine Supreme Inner Self by Means of True and Spiritual) Meditation Is the (Great and Single) Purpose of your life (and, indeed, the Very Truth In Which you are, now and always, deeply Concentrated), you are Hereby Given the Name Dhyanananda.

In the Path (Sphere, Tradition, Line, and Lineage) of Yoga, you (by Virtue of this Declaration) will (or, by Right, can) henceforth be Known (Called, Addressed, or Referred to) as (or by the Name of) Dhyanananda.

You are a True Bearer of the Wealth of the Knowledge of Siddha Yoga,[6] as It is Given at (Shree) Gurudev Ashram. The Kundalini Shakti, Which (by Grace) Gives (Grants, or Bestows) and Accomplishes Siddha Yoga, Is Actively at Work in you.

Likewise, you are a True Knower (or Actual, and potentially Perfect, Realizer) of Vedanta. The (Divine Supreme Inner) Self, Which Is the Secret (and the Ultimate Truth) of Vedanta, and Which Is the Very Basis (Foundation, or Root) of True Religion (or the Way of Truth), and Which (or Perfect Realization of Which, or Perfectly Absorbed Identification With Which) Is the (True, and Ultimate) Goal of human life, has been Awakened, and Is Awake, in you by Means of the Active Work of the (Kundalini) Shakti (or Divine Power).

"Only one who has actually seen (or experienced) a particular something can testify (or bear true witness) to it (or speak with authority relative to its existence and its nature, and otherwise affirm, authenticate, certify, prove, manifest, show, or demonstrate it)." Based on this Principle (or the obvious reasonableness of this Argument), you (because of your direct Experience and Knowledge of Kundalini Shakti Meditation and, Thereby, of the Divine Supreme Inner Self) have, in accordance with Tradition, both the (Hereby Affirmed) Actual Ability and the Inherent (and Hereby Affirmed) Right to Initiate, or Cause, (True and Spiritual) Meditation in others (or, altogether, to Teach, Initiate, Establish, Guide, and Awaken others in the Practice, the Process, and the, Ultimately, Perfect Realization of Siddha Yoga Meditation, or True and Spiritual Meditation on, and, Ultimately, Perfect Realization of, the Divine Supreme Inner Self by Means of the Kundalini Shakti Transmitted, and Directly Activated, by you).

With an Authority based on this same Principle (of Experience itself), the Scriptures Testify and Declare (and I, likewise, Affirm to you) that, if you have Faith (or genuine Trust) in the Guru, and if you (persistently) Meditate on your (Inherent) Oneness with the Divine Being, and if you Maintain an "Equal Eye" of Regard toward all human beings, the Goddess, Chitti Kundalini,[7] will (always) Help (and Support) you Fully, and She will not only Grant you the appropriate (or right) enjoyment of (human) life (or the appropriate natural, or ordinary, fulfillments of human life), but She will also "Fill" (or Perfectly Fulfill) you with (the Gift of Ultimate, Perfect, and Final) Liberation.

Therefore, May you (by the Grace of the Goddess, Chitti Kundalini) Realize (or Obtain and Achieve) Perfect Absorption In, and Perfect Identification, and Perfect Sameness, With, the Divine Being, and This by Means of the Perfect Fulfillment of your Primary Duty, Which Is to Worship the Divine Being by Meditating on your (Inherent) Identity As the Divine Supreme Inner Self. Thus (Saying This), I Give you my Blessing.

Kundalini Yoga[8] is a possibility for every one, since the Kundalini Shakti (Which Is the Active Source, and the Divine Doer, of Kundalini Yoga) Exists (latently) in every one, and every one (and every thing) exists (or resides) in (or is alive, or existing, in, As, and by Means of) the (Divine) Kundalini Shakti. And Meditation (on the Divine Supreme Inner Self) by Means of the Kundalini Shakti (Awakened by the Guru's Grace) Is (necessarily) the Primary Duty of every one (because every one Originates from the Divine Source, and, therefore, every one owes, or must render, surrender, and return, his or her Divinely Originated existence to, the Kundalini Shakti, Which Is the Divine Source-Power, and Which Is the Way to the Divine Supreme Inner Self-Source of all). Therefore, (I Hereby Declare that) you have the Inherent Right and the Actual Ability to Cause (or, altogether, to Teach, Initiate, Establish, and Guide Kundalini Yoga) Meditation (or the Practice and the Process of Kundalini Shakti Meditation) in any one and everyone (and, Thus and Thereby, to Awaken any one and everyone to and As the Divine Supreme Inner Self of all).

> *Swami Muktananda,*
> *Thana District,*
> *Maharashtra State,*
> *India*

India, 1970

III.

Via His public letter of Acknowledgement and Proclamation, Baba Muktananda Offered Me the traditional Name "Dhyanananda", which means "One Who Realizes (or, Has Realized) The Divine Being-Existence, Consciousness, And Bliss Through Deeply Meditative self-Surrender", or "One Whose Bliss Is In Absolute Surrender To His Innermost Self", or, most properly, "One Who Realizes (or, Has Realized) The Divine Self-Condition (Of Unalloyed Bliss, Infinite Consciousness, And Eternal Being-Existence) Through True And Spiritual Meditation On (And, Altogether, One-Pointed And Absolute self-Surrender To) His Own True (or, Divine Supreme Inner) Self". And it was Baba Muktananda's explicit Intention that I should, by means of this Name, be approached and addressed as a Spiritual Teacher (or Siddha-Guru), openly Functioning as a Transmission-Master of Kundalini Yoga (and of Siddha Yoga).

Baba Muktananda's explicit (written) Acknowledgement and Proclamation that Meditation had already Fulfilled itself to the degree that I (by virtue of true and advanced Yogic and Spiritual Awakening, including Yogic Self-Realization via fifth stage conditional Nirvikalpa Samadhi) could formally be Acknowledged and Proclaimed to have the Inherent Right to Teach others implicitly Conferred upon Me the Title or Designation of "Yogi" (and He otherwise verbally and directly referred to Me by this Title or Designation in public conversation during the same period in which His letter of Acknowledgement and Proclamation was written). Likewise, and altogether, by Means of its clear implications (and, also, the Granting of a Name formulated in the traditional sannyasin manner[9]), Baba Muktananda's public letter of Acknowledgement and Proclamation tacitly Conferred sannyasa diksha[10] (or initiation into the formal renunciate life) on Me, and the perpetual option of formal sannyasa (which I, in due course, Embraced).

Baba Muktananda's public letter of Acknowledgement and Proclamation simply stands as a Free Gift. It is a Sign and an Instrument of His Spiritual Blessing. It was Given to Me Freely, as an Acknowledgement of My Freedom, and it was specifically Intended that I use it Freely (and Teach Freely), in any manner that I Choose.

The primary Intention of Baba Muktananda's letter was to Affirm and Acknowledge My advanced Yogic and Spiritual Awakening, and, on that basis, to formally Convey to Me (or Acknowledge in Me) the Right to Teach, and thus to Function as Spiritual Transmission-Master (or Siddha-Guru) in relation to others. And His ultimate Intention, fully and openly Communicated to Me in many ways, was that I simply Accept His Acknowledgement and His Blessing, and that I go on to Live and Teach in Freedom. And This is precisely what I Did from the day I Received this Acknowledgement and Blessing.

IV.

The "Naming" Letter (and all of Baba Muktananda's Affirmation and Acknowledgement of Me) changed nothing. It did not represent status to Me (such that to accept it should change My life or My manner). Rather, it simply Affirmed and Acknowledged what was already the case. Therefore, the Name ("Dhyanananda"), the Title ("Yogi"), and the "Right to Teach" were indeed Accepted by Me, but simply as Blessings (and, truly, as a kind of Ending, or Completeness, relative to the past, and what had been Realized in the past).

It can (and, rightly, should) be assumed that I, from the day of Baba Muktananda's "Naming" letter, was, according to tradition, formally Acknowledged and Confirmed as a Spiritually Active Yogi and a Spiritual Transmission-Master (or Siddha-Guru), with the Characteristics of a True and Free Renunciate (and with the perpetual option of formal sannyasa), and with the Inherent (and the traditional) Right to Teach (and Thereby to Initiate, Bless, and Awaken) others, and, likewise, with the Inherent (and the traditional) Right to Affirm, Acknowledge, Confirm, or otherwise Proclaim the state or stage of practice or Realization demonstrated by any others. However, I simply continued (spontaneously) in the progressively unfolding drama of Impulse and developing Realization that had occupied Me since My infancy.

It was not until another full year had passed (and the Great Process had Developed in Me apart from Baba Muktananda's physical company, and beyond the particular Yogic Designs Affirmed as Truth by Him and His fifth stage tradition[11]) that the Impulse Awake in Me at Birth (or the Active Impulse toward the Re-Awakening of Perfectly Subjective Divine Self-Realization, made necessary from My infancy) was Fulfilled in Its Inherent Perfection (on September 10, 1970).[12] And when I began (from then, progressively, at first reservedly, then openly and formally,

41

Adi Da with devotees in Los Angeles, 1973

and, at last, Fully) to Teach,[13] it was in the Western world, where neither renunciation, nor Spiritual Yoga, nor the Guru-devotee tradition, nor Perfectly Subjective Divine Self-Realization was (or is) understood or even honored.

My Teaching Work did not truly begin (as a Great Intention, beyond rudimentary Yogic and Instructional activities) until Perfectly Subjective Divine Self-Realization Spontaneously Re-Awakened in My case, followed by the Spontaneous Great Siddhis associated with My own unique Teaching and Blessing Work.[14]

And the Way that I Taught was (and is) the Way of the Heart (Which is the Name I have Given to My own unique Revelation of the Means and the Process of Most Ultimate, and Inherently Most Perfect, Divine Self-Realization).[15]

My manner of Teaching involved Free or Spontaneous Identification With those who came to Me, and Freely Responsive Participation in their problems and their conditions of living. That Teaching Work developed among ordinary people (mostly Americans and Europeans), who were devoted to the Omega culture[16] of the first three stages of life. Therefore, during My years of Teaching Work, I did not feel it would be appropriate or useful for Me to assume either a traditional monastic habit of living or any other outward formalities that might be associated with traditional renunciation (or that would otherwise, in effect, Affirm My Retirement from all Teaching Obligations). My Intention as Teacher was simply and Freely to Do all that I could possibly Do to make My Teaching Work both Complete and Fruitful.

My Teaching Work (in its most active form) did in fact become Complete (or Full) on January 11, 1986.[17] On that day, and from that day, many Signs of that Fullness and Completeness (or Siddhi) Appeared Spontaneously and progressively in My bodily human Form and in My Work. As part of this Appearance of Signs, on April 11, 1986, I (Spontaneously, and formally) Embraced (or Confirmed and Affirmed) the Sign of sannyasa (or the formal renunciate

The Mountain Of Attention, 1986

life), and, thus, I formally Embraced the formal habit, discipline, outward mode, and circumstance of a Swami (or one who disciplines and transcends the body-mind in a formal renunciate manner). By these means, I formally (and in the traditional manner) Proclaimed and Demonstrated My own Free Life (as One Who is not and cannot be confounded by the world). And I Did this Freely, for the sake of all practitioners of the Way of the Heart (in order to Inspire True and Free renunciation[18] in them and to advance their understanding of My "Radical"[19] Wisdom-Teaching).

After April 11, 1986, and in order to more fully Embrace the traditional Sign of tapas (or austerity),[20] I Wandered among My devotees (and the public) in America and Europe. While I Wandered, I Did Penance (and Accepted every kind of abuse) in My own Body for the sake of the Purification and Spiritual Awakening of the entire world. Then, on July 17, 1986, I (Spontaneously) Relinquished all limiting association with the exclusively Hindu tradition of sannyasa (or, that is to say, I formally Confirmed My Stand as a formal sannyasin and a True and Free Renunciate, but Most Fully, in the characteristic manner of a True and Free Avadhoota,[21] or a Perfectly Free Man, without property, and Inherently Free in relation to all the conditions of human existence, and Free of all limiting associations with the Great Tradition of mankind).

With this Signal of Perfect Renunciation (on July 17, 1986), My apparent (or apparently more extreme) Austerities, or the Acts of Penance and voluntary abasement of this Body (even in the form of all the years of My Ordeal as Teacher), were (in Truth) Ended and Made Complete (and it only remained for others to understand and honor the, from then, and now, and forever hereafter, non-necessity for Me to Teach by Submission and to Serve by excess of Austerity, or by Penance, or by abasement of My Person, or by the Acceptance, on My Person, of abuse, exploitation, neglect, or inappropriate approach).

Adi Da Purnashram, September, 1994

V.

In order further to Affirm and further to Demonstrate the Perfect Sufficiency of Divine Self-Realization (and in order further to Affirm the Necessity, the Rightness, and the Fruitfulness of My own unique, and even lifelong, Signs of Real self-Renunciation, or True ego-Renunciation, and Real self-Transcendence, or True ego-Transcendence), I Spontaneously (and formally) Re-Affirmed the Perfectly True and Fullest Free sannyasin Form of Renunciation (or the Inherent, and Inherently self-Transcending, and Inherently Perfect, Renunciation that is characteristic of an Avadhoota), at Adi Da Purnashram, the Island of Naitauba, My Great Sannyasin Hermitage Ashram in Fiji, on December 27, 1987.[22]

Nevertheless, My devotees continued to be slow in understanding and truly and fully responding to My Divine "Emergence" here. Therefore, it was required, for a time, that I continue to "Explain all", and even, to a degree, to Teach My devotees by Submission to them, and also to continue to endure even their abuse of Me, their exploitation of Me, their neglect of Me, and their inappropriate approach to Me. This continued for another nearly nine years, until, on September 7, 1994, My Acceptance of all of that Suddenly and Spontaneously Ceased, and I Knew I had forever Said and Done Enough (Such that there was not even any Motion in Me to Say or Do any More). My Revelation Work had Suddenly become Complete, for all time, and I (Spontaneously, and Finally) Came To Rest in My Eternal Hermitage of Heart-Seclusion (only, from then, and forever, to Awaken all beings by Mere and Constant Blessing, "Bright").

Therefore, now that I have Done (or Suffered) all that was necessary for Me to Do (or Suffer) as Teacher and Revealer in a Struggle with would-be devotees and the world, I will not hereafter Associate with that Struggle, but I have Retired from that Struggle, Satisfied that all My Teaching Work, and even all My Revelation Work, Is Full and Complete (and that, by Fullest Submission, I have, Most

Adi Da Purnashram, 1994

Fully and Most Finally, Said and Done and Firmly Established all that I could possibly have Said and Done and Firmly Established, and all that was necessary for Me to Say and Do and Firmly Establish, in order, now, and for all time to come, to Most Fully and Most Finally, and Firmly, Introduce the Great Opportunity to the total human world, in all the stages of life, and in order, now, and for all time to come, to Most Fully and Most Finally, and Firmly, Provide the True, and Most Perfect, and Utterly Complete Way Of God, Truth, and Reality to the total human world, in all the stages of life, and in order, now, and for all time to come, to Most Fully and Most Finally, and Firmly, Establish the True, and Most Perfect, and Utterly Complete Way of God, Truth, and Reality for the Liberating Sake of the total human world, in all the stages of life).

Now I Live in relative Seclusion, and yet always Accessible to My rightly prepared formal renunciate devotees (and, as I Will, to others of My rightly prepared devotees, and even to whomever I Will), for the Sake of all My devotees (and for the Sake of even all beings).[23] The extraordinary manner of My years of Teaching Work and Revelation Work, and My characteristic, and always continuing, Freedom to Work as I Will in relation to My devotees, require no conventional justification. I Make and Bear only My own Signs. I will always Bless every one and all. And I will always remain Accessible to those of My formal renunciate devotees (and, perhaps, others of My devotees, as I Will) who approach Me altogether rightly, Full of Devotional feeling for Me, Fully resorting and surrendering to Me, Fully prepared for intensive self-discipline in response to Me,[24] and for self-surrendering, self-forgetting, and self-transcending service to Me, and for Right, and True, and Truly Spiritual meditation on Me, and, altogether, for Right, and True, and Truly Spiritual use of My Company. Nevertheless, I will not Submit to be the Teacher again, except that I will always Speak, even if by Silence, to (or, otherwise, for the Sake of) all who will listen to Me.

Adi Da Purnashram, 1994

VI.

I long ago passed beyond meditation (or "Dhyana", from which the Name "Dhyanananda" is derived). Likewise, I long ago passed beyond all identification with any separate tradition or traditional limitation. I have Freely Established and Completely Fulfilled the (Ultimately, Most Perfect) Way of the Heart, Which is the Way that only I can Reveal and Give. And the Way of the Heart (first Established and Fulfilled by Me, and, now and forever hereafter, Revealed and Given by Me) does not depend on the conventional traditional supports, limits, or vows. Nevertheless, I Freely Embrace and Bless <u>all</u> traditions, East and West.

My own and Original (and Divinely Self-Revealed) Name is simply "Da" ("The One Who Gives"), and "Adi Da" ("The First, The One and Only, The Giver of All to all") [25]. I Am the "Bright" ("Avabhasa"), Self-Existing As the Eternally Free and Eternally "Bright" Divine Heart (or "Hridayam") Itself, and Self-Radiant As the Eternally Free and Eternally "Bright" Divine Love-Bliss (or "Love-Ananda") Itself. Therefore, I Am "Santosha" (Inherently and Perfectly Satisfied and Contented, Inherently and Perfectly Free of all seeking, Inherently and Perfectly Free of all separateness, and Inherently and Perfectly Complete). I simply <u>Am</u>, Prior to Dhyana (or attention on any object or state). My Only "Practice" [26] is Inherent, and Inherently Most Perfect, Realization of Reality Itself, or Perfectly Subjective Transcendental (and Inherently Spiritual) Divine Self-Abiding, Feeling or Being As Consciousness Itself, Prior to attention to objects or states, Prior to attention itself, Spontaneously Recognizing [27] (<u>As</u> the Perfectly Subjective "Bright", Transcendental, and Inherently Spiritual, Divine Self) whatever apparently arises and, therefore, never stopping "Natural" (Sahaj) [28] or Native Self-Abiding, but simply Standing As the Inherent Love-Bliss of Consciousness Itself.

Just as I Took the Divinely Self-Revealed Name "Bubba Free John"[29] when My Sacrificial Teaching Work began in Its Fullness, and just as the Name "Da" was Divinely Self-Revealed and Confessed to all (replacing "Bubba Free John" with "Da Free John" when the time was right), so also, now that all My Teaching Work, and all My Revelation Work, is Complete, and I simply Stand Free, it is necessary that all My devotees (or all those who practice the only-by-Me Revealed and Given Way of the Heart), and also all others, rightly and fully understand Me by Name. Therefore, it has become appropriate for My devotees, and also all others, to (generally) refer to Me simply by My Principal Revelation-Name, "Da", and by My Fully Elaborated Principal Revelation-Name, "Adi Da", and by such Titles and Designations (which I will indicate) that properly Express and Affirm only My present and future Relationship and Stand relative to practitioners of the only-by-Me Revealed and Given Way of the Heart and relative to the total world.

Every one should refer to Me in a wholly appropriate and right manner. And practitioners of the Way of the Heart should both refer and relate to Me in a manner that reflects a right and truly responsive Devotional Acknowledgement of Me. Therefore, the present and future use of Names, Titles, and Designations in reference to Me should also serve and express the intention of practitioners of the Way of the Heart (and even all others) to relinquish otherwise (or now) inappropriate habits of relating to Me that may have developed in the years of My Teaching Work (or that do not express the right and fullest understanding of Me and all My Work).

VII.

I Am Retired from My Teaching Work (or that part of My Great Work which originally required active and most humanly intentional Submission to would-be devotees and the world). My Word of Teaching is Full and Given. I have Spontaneously Entered into a Supremely Free Disposition, without My originally Presumed Teaching Obligations. In that Disposition, I will simply Abide at Adi Da Purnashram (Naitauba), and I may sometimes also Wander (even every where). I Am Beyond concerns and attachments and dissociative intentions relative to the body-mind, others, and the world. I Am Beyond meditation. I Am the Ishta,[30] or the "Chosen One", of all My true listening devotees, all My true hearing devotees, and all My true see-ing devotees.[31] I Am Beyond ordinary vows and rules. I Am Beyond limitations. I Am Beyond limited and limiting tradi-tions. I Am Beyond the search by self-indulgence and the search by strategic (or goal-directed) renunciation. I Am celi-bate. I Am not celibate. I Am Free of the cumulative burdens associated with apparent action. I Am Beyond the necessity and the concern to Teach. My Only Vow and Obligation Is the Purpose Who I Am. Therefore, I Am Avadhoota, Free As My Self, Free Forever for the Sake of all and All.

I have Transcended Dhyana (or meditation) through seventh stage Sahaj Samadhi (or Inherent, or Native, and Inherently Most Perfect, and Perfectly Subjective, and Utterly Spontaneous, Transcendental, Inherently Spiritual, and Divine Self-Realization).[32] Baba Muktananda Himself, in His "Naming" letter, Declared that Dhyana had already become much advanced, and significantly Fulfilled, in My case. However, I did not begin to Teach, formally and openly, until the Fulfillment of My Meditation was utterly (or Inherently Most Perfectly) Demonstrated (even <u>beyond</u> the ascending Yogic Process of the fifth stage of life, and beyond the limits of even the sixth stage of life) at the Vedanta Temple, on September 10, 1970. Therefore, when I finally began to Teach, My Teaching Work was based on the Siddhi (or Divine Power and Impulse) Re-Awakened in seventh stage Sahaj Samadhi (or Perfectly Subjective and Inherently Most Perfectly Full Spiritual and Transcendental Divine Self-Realization, Which characterizes the seventh stage of life, and Which was the Most Ultimate Fulfillment of My Practice), rather than on the basis of Baba Muktananda's earlier Acknowledgement, which was based on My Attainment of advanced fifth stage Yogic and Spiritual Signs of the meditative ascent of attention (including temporary meditative ascent beyond the body-mind, and to utterly ascended Realization of the Divine Oneness, or fifth stage Yogic Self-Realization, in fifth stage conditional Nirvikalpa Samadhi). Therefore, I never Taught as "Dhyananda".

However, just before He wrote Me His letter of Acknowledgement and Empowerment in 1969, Baba Muktananda (through His then secretary and interpreter, Pratibha Trivedi, known at that time as Amma, later Swami Prajnananda) happily and spontaneously Offered to Me the Name "Love-Ananda", which means "One Who Is The Divine Love-Bliss", or "One Who Is, and Manifests, The Divine Love-Bliss", or, most properly, "One Who Is The Inherent Bliss, Infinite Consciousness, And Eternal Being-Existence Of The Transcendental, And Inherently Spiritual, Divine Person And Self-Condition, Manifesting As Infinite, Or Boundless, Love-Bliss, And As Universal, And All-Blissful, Love Toward all beings". Therefore, the Name "Love-Ananda" indicates That Which Is the Ultimate Fulfillment of Dhyana (or of any and all forms of practice that seek Spiritual and Transcendental Divine Realization of God, Truth, Reality, or the Real and True Self).

From the moment I heard this Name "Love-Ananda", I felt the Blessing of Baba Muktananda, and I Accepted the Name as Baba Muktananda's basic and original and spontaneous heart-Intention toward Me.

I presumed the letter of Acknowledgement which was to follow would simply be a Re-Affirmation of this Name "Love-Ananda" and a formal Acknowledgement of My Right to

Teach. Therefore, the Name "Dhyanananda" was unexpected, but I Received it happily, and I was also amused by the Mysteriousness of Baba Muktananda's Gift of two Names (one Offered secretly, and the other Offered publicly).

Then, approximately one year after these "Naming" incidents, Dhyana (or self-Transcending Meditation on the Spiritual, Transcendental, and Divine Self-Condition of Reality) was Spontaneously (and Inherently Most Perfectly) Fulfilled in Me. The One Who was Named "Dhyanananda" (because of His Effective <u>Meditation</u> on and in and As the One Spiritual, Transcendental, and Divine Being-Existence, and Consciousness, and Love-Bliss) Realized His Inherent, and Inherently Perfect, Identity As Love-Ananda, the Inherent Love-Bliss of the One, and Perfectly Subjective, Transcendental, Inherently Spiritual, and Divine Self-Existence. Finally, in the spring of 1986, nearly seventeen years after I first Received His Gift of two Names, I formally and Freely Accepted the Name "Love-Ananda" that was spontaneously Offered to Me by Baba Muktananda in 1969.

In His "Naming" letter, Baba Muktananda does not directly <u>Refer</u> to Me by the Name "Dhyanananda". He simply States that I am "Hereby Given the Name Dhyanananda" and that, "in the Path (Sphere, Tradition, Line, and Lineage) of Yoga", I "will (or, by Right, can) henceforth be Known (Called, Addressed, or Referred to) as (or by the Name of) Dhyanananda". If Baba Muktananda's own "Path" is understood, in this context, to be that of "Yoga" (in the ascending or fifth stage tradition), then, in some sense, I "became Known" as Dhyanananda "in the Path of Yoga" (because people in Baba Muktananda's circle knew He had Given Me this Name).

However, the Spiritual Process continued to Develop in My case, beyond the (fifth stage) context of the Yoga defined and experienced and Taught by Baba Muktananda. Indeed, great (comparative) differences (or characteristic and necessary distinctions) between My expressed (seventh stage) "Point of View" and that expressed by Baba

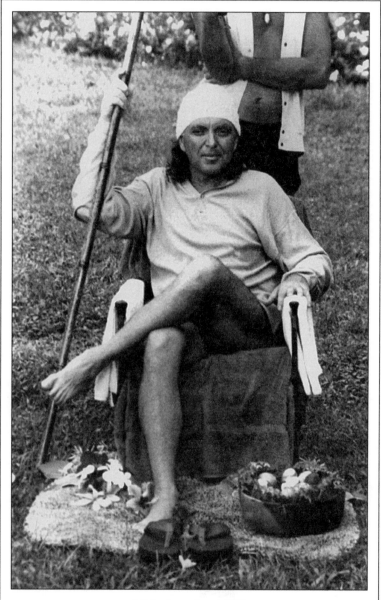

Adi Da Purnashram, 1986

Muktananda (typically, in fifth stage terms) developed as a result of the Spontaneous Re-Awakening that Occurred in My case in the year following Baba Muktananda's Acknowledgement of Me. Therefore, after the Great Event at the Vedanta Temple in 1970, and the subsequent publication of My Heart-Confessing Word, the outer relationship (or outer communicative exchange) between Baba Muktananda and Me progressively came to an end.

In any case, not only was I Given the Name "Dhyanananda", but I was also Given the Name "Love-Ananda". My formal (or public) Acceptance of Baba Muktananda's "Naming-Blessing" came long after Dhyana was replaced by the Realization of Love-Ananda. Therefore, it is most appropriate for Me to Accept the Name "Love-Ananda" (which was the first Name to be Given, and which corresponds to That Which has Most Ultimately been Realized). Likewise, the Name "Love-Ananda" (Given Spontaneously and, as it were, for Free) can be Freely used, however I Will.

The Name "Love-Ananda" combines both Western and Eastern words or Names, thus transcending either category, or the limitations of both Omega and Alpha.[33] Clearly, the Name "Dhyanananda" was not the one Baba Muktananda originally Conceived for Me, but it was Chosen later, perhaps because the Name "Love-Ananda" was considered to be too unconventional by those who heard of it, or perhaps simply because of My internal experience of an elaborate technical Revelation of the Process of Dhyana while Sitting privately with Baba Muktananda in the morning hours immediately before He wrote His "Naming" letter to Me. In any case, the Name "Love-Ananda" was Communicated to Me first, and it is the Name I am moved to Accept as the Free and Loving Gift of Baba Muktananda. (Therefore, although the Name "Dhyanananda" was also Given, it should be regarded, simply, as one of My uncommonly Given historical Names, and one that, like the more common Names given to Me at birth, was, ultimately, superseded.)

The Mountain Of Attention, 1995

VIII.

Aham Da Asmi.[34] I Am Da. I Am the True Divine Person, the One and Only Self of All and all. I Am (now, and forever hereafter) Manifesting As the Da Avatar, Who Is the First, the Complete, the Last, and the Only Avataric Manifestation of Da, or the Divine Intervention As the True Heart-Master of all. Therefore, I Am the Da Avatar, the Realizer, the Revealer, and the Revelation of the True Divine Person, Who Is the One and Only God, Truth, and Reality. And, now that all My Teaching Work and all My Revelation Work is Full and Complete, I simply (and forever) Abide at and in front of the Heart of all beings. Therefore, for all who have Found Me (and become My devotees), I Am the One and Only Ishta-Guru (the First and True and Eternal Murti,[35] the Threshold Personality, and the forever Living Sign and Revelation of the True Divine Person).

Now that My Self-Revelation is Complete, all My listening devotees, all My hearing devotees, all My seeing devotees, and all of the general public should address and refer to Me As I <u>Am</u>. They should, primarily, and generally, address and refer to Me by My Divinely Self-Revealed (and culturally universal) Name "Da", which means, and indicates, that My Work Is That of the Giving Giver, and I <u>Am</u> the One Who Gives. And, as a further acknowledgement and indication that I Am the Da Avatar (Inherently Identical to the Divine Person, Who <u>Is</u> Da), and that I Am the First ("Adi"), the Complete, the Last, and the Only Avataric Manifestation of Da (or of the Divine Intervention As the True Heart-Master of all), the address or reference to Me by the Name "Da" should, generally, be preceded by the Descriptive Name "Adi" (which means, and indicates, that I Am the First Person, the Original Person, the Primordial One, the Source, the One and Only Self, the True Divine Person).

All My listening devotees, all My hearing devotees, and all My seeing devotees should reserve the use of My Single Name "Da" for occasions of meditation on Me by Name, and for moments of spontaneous ecstatic devotional exclamation, or for moments of spontaneous ecstatic devotional Invocation of Me, or, otherwise, for formal sacramental use. And, because all My devotees reserve My Single Name "Da" for uniquely sacred use only, all of the general public should also, except perhaps for occasions of unique, ecstatic address or reference to Me, only address or refer to Me as "Adi Da", or, most properly, as any of the forms of My Names I will now Indicate, combined, as I will now also Indicate, with appropriate formal Titles, or Designations, or Descriptive References.

Secondarily (or occasionally, as an alternative to the Name "Da", and the full reference "Adi Da"), all My listening devotees, all My hearing devotees, all My seeing devotees, and all of the general public may address and refer to Me by the Names "Da Avabhasa" and "Avabhasa Da" and "Da Avabhasa (The 'Bright')" and "Adi Da Avabhasa" and "Avabhasa Adi Da" (all of which mean, and indicate, "The 'Bright'", or the Divine Love-Bliss Itself), and "Da Love-Ananda" and "Love-Ananda Da" and "Adi Da Love-Ananda" and "Love-Ananda Adi Da" (all of which mean, and indicate, "The Divine Love-Bliss", or the "Bright" Itself), and "Da Santosha" and "Santosha Da" and "Adi Da Santosha" and "Santosha Adi Da" (all of which mean, and indicate, "The 'Bright' and Eternal and Always Already Non-Separate Person of Divine and Inherent Completeness, Divine Self-Satisfaction, Divine Self-Contentedness, or Perfect Searchlessness, Which Completeness, Self-Satisfaction, Self-Contentedness, or Perfect Searchlessness Is the Inherent Characteristic of the Divine Love-Bliss, or the 'Bright' Itself, and Which 'Bright' and Eternal and Always Already Non-Separate Person Is the One and Only Self, the True and Only Divine Person, the Only and Absolute Self-Condition of All and all"). Therefore, because each and all of these (secondary) Names of Mine mean and indicate That Which I Give, and That Which I <u>Am</u>, they may be used freely (but secondarily) in address or reference to Me by all of My listening devotees, and all of My hearing devotees, and all of My seeing devotees, and all of the general public.

I am a naturalized Free citizen of Fiji, and I have been given Names, Titles, and honorific Designations by the native citizens of Fiji. Therefore, in keeping with those Names, Titles, and honorific Designations, all My listening devotees, all My hearing devotees, all My seeing devotees, and all of the general public, even every where, may also (secondarily) address and refer to Me as "Dau Loloma", or, more properly, "Adi Dau Loloma", or, most properly, "Turaga [Adi] Dau Loloma", or, alternatively, "Tui [Adi] Dau Loloma", or "[Turaga, or, alternatively, Tui] Dau Loloma Da", or "[Turaga, or Tui] Adi Dau Loloma Da", or "[Turaga, or Tui] Dau Loloma Adi Da", or "Naitauba [Adi] Dau Loloma", or "[Adi] Dau Loloma Naitauba" (all of which mean, and indicate, that I Am the Divine Adept of the Divine Love), or, more formally, as "[Adi] Dau Loloma Vunirarama" (which means, and indicates, that I Am the Divine Adept of the Divine Love, and the Self-Radiant Divine Source of the Divine "Brightness"), or, most formally, as any appropriate combination of the Name "[Adi] Dau Loloma Vunirarama" with, as above, the formal Title or Designation "Turaga", or "Tui", or "Naitauba", or even any appropriate combination of the Name "[Adi] Dau Loloma Vunirarama" with any formal Title or Designation, in any language, that may otherwise be used in appropriate reference to Me.[36]

All My listening devotees, all My hearing devotees, all My seeing devotees, and all of the general public may also (secondarily) address and refer to Me by adding either the Name "Hridayam" or the Title, or Designation, "Hridaya" (both of which mean, and indicate, "The Inherently and

The Mountain Of Attention, 1995

Perfectly Free and Divine Heart Itself") and/or the Title, or Designation, "Avadhoota" (which means, and indicates, "The One Who Is Inherently and Perfectly Free and Divine") to any or all of My Names, and Titles, or Designations, because I <u>Am</u> the Divine Heart Itself, and I <u>Am</u> the Divine Freedom Itself, and As Such I Am to be addressed, and referred to, and Realized.[37]

Only My Spiritually Awakened devotees can (because they both hear Me and see Me) <u>most</u> <u>fully</u> Acknowledge and Realize Me as the True Heart-Master (or Hridaya-Samartha Sat-Guru). Nevertheless, I Am the True Heart-Master (One and Only) of <u>all</u> My devotees (and of even <u>all</u> beings). For this reason, the Title or Designation "True Heart-Master" (or, simply, "Heart-Master") is an appropriate formal reference that My any devotee (or, indeed, any one at all) may apply in reference or address to Me.

In fullest right address or reference to Me, all My listening devotees, all My hearing devotees, all My seeing devotees, and all of the general public should generally address and refer to Me as "Adi Da", followed (or, otherwise, preceded) by the Descriptive Reference "The Da Avatar" (or secondarily, "The Hridaya Avatara", or "The Avabhasa Avatara", or "The Love-Ananda Avatara", or "The Santosha Avatara"), and they may also freely combine the Title, or Designation, "Avatar(a)" with My primary and secondary Names, because I Am the Eternally Free-Standing and (now, and forever hereafter) Always Presently "Emerging" Divine World-Teacher, Given, as a Grace, to all, and Always Giving Grace to all, and I Am the Expected late-time God-Man, the Complete and all-Completing Avataric Incarnation, the True Ultimate Man-Born Descent of Divine and all-Liberating Grace every where, anciently and always, Promised for the dark epoch, which dark epoch, or late-time, Must, by My "Heroic"[38] Spiritual Intervention, Be, More and More, Until Most Perfectly, Restored at Heart to the Divine Self-"Brightness".[39]

In addition, whenever I am addressed or referred to by or among My listening devotees, My hearing devotees, My seeing devotees, and the informed public, any one of the many possible (and appropriately formal) variations on these Names (and others that may properly be attributed or applied to Me) and these Titles or Designations (or other Titles or Designations that are traditionally suggested to be used to address or refer to the True Avatar, or to the True God-Man, or to the True World-Teacher, or to the True Divine Ishta of devotees, or to the True Realizer, Spiritual Master, and Sat-Guru) may, in any particular moment, be appropriate.

Let each of My listening devotees, My hearing devotees, and My seeing devotees choose which of all these forms (and all other possibly appropriate forms or variations) of address or reference to Me is most congenial and appropriate in the context of any moment. And all others should likewise respect (and be guided in their use of) this Order of My Free Names.

Notes to the Text of
"The Order of My Free Names"

1. By the Designation "Yogic Siddha", Avatara Adi Da acknowledges Swami Muktananda as an Adept of all the extraordinary psycho-physical and Spiritual processes of the paths of Yoga. "Baba" (father) is a traditional term of both affection and respect for one's Guru, and it is the name Avatara Adi Da used in addressing Swami Muktananda and that He still uses sometimes in referring to the Swami. Avatara Adi Da has called Swami Muktananda His principal Spirit-Baptizer, because the Yogic Siddha's Company and Touch were directly associated with Bhagavan Adi Da's Realization of fifth stage conditional Nirvikalpa Samadhi, to which He refers further on in this paragraph.

2. Fifth stage conditional Nirvikalpa Samadhi is an isolated, or periodic, Realization of the ascent of attention beyond all conditional manifestation into the formless Matrix of the Spirit-Current, or Divine Light, infinitely above the world, the body, and the mind. And, like all the forms of Samadhi that may be Realized previous to Divine Self-Realization, conditional Nirvikalpa Samadhi is a forced and temporary state of attention (or, more precisely, of the suspension of attention). It is produced by manipulation of attention and of the body-mind, and is thus incapable of being maintained when attention returns, as it inevitably does, to the states of the body-mind.

Traditionally, fifth stage conditional Nirvikalpa Samadhi is the goal of the many schools of Yogic ascent. In the Way of the Heart, while it is understood that fifth stage conditional Nirvikalpa Samadhi is not Divine Self-Realization, nevertheless, it is a possible, though not necessary, sign of developing Spiritual maturity.

Avatara Adi Da's Realization of fifth stage conditional Nirvikalpa Samadhi was remarkable, not only because of the intensity of His Spiritual practice that preceded it, but also because of the rapidity with which His Spiritual practice showed this traditional sign of advancement. He was Served in the Realization of fifth stage conditional Nirvikalpa Samadhi by the Yogic initiation of three Great Yogic Siddhas: Swami Muktananda, described above; Sri Rang Avadhoot (1898-1968), whose brief glance also immediately preceded Bhagavan Adi Da's Recollection of the Divine State via fifth stage conditional Nirvikalpa Samadhi; and the then late but still Spiritually active Swami Nityananda who, even after Bhagavan Adi Da's Realization of fifth stage conditional Nirvikalpa Samadhi on this occasion, continued (by direct Spiritual visitations) to urge and inspire Him toward the ultimate and Perfect Realization of Spiritual, Transcendental, and Divine Truth and Freedom.

For a further discussion of fifth stage conditional Nirvikalpa Samadhi, please see chapter forty-three of *The Dawn Horse Testament Of Adi Da*. See also Appendix B: The Seven Stages of Life, pp. 155-58.

3. "Siddhi" is Sanskrit for "power", or "accomplishment". The Yogic siddhis Avatara Adi Da refers to here are also traditionally called "ordinary", or "natural", siddhis. In traditional paths, such lesser siddhis are typically either sought or shunned. In the Way of the Heart, they may arise as signs of the purification and enlivening of the body-mind by the Radiant Heart-Blessing of Bhagavan Adi Da. If they appear, as they did in Avatara Adi Da's own Sadhana, the practitioner of the Way of the Heart simply observes, understands, and transcends them, like all other arising experiences, knowledge, and capabilities, and neither exploits nor strategically avoids them.

When capitalized in Avatara Adi Da's Wisdom-Teaching, "Siddhi" is the Spiritual, Transcendental, and Divine Awakening-Power that He spontaneously and effortlessly Transmits to all. It is the Maha-Siddhi, the Great, or Ultimate, Siddhi, the Power of the Heart, or Awakened Consciousness.

4. Avatara Adi Da uses the phrase "Most Perfect(ly)" in the sense of "Absolutely Perfect(ly)". Similarly, the phrase "Most Ultimate(ly)" is equivalent to "Absolutely Ultimate(ly)".

In the sixth stage of life and the seventh stage of life, What is Realized (Consciousness Itself) is Perfect (and Ultimate). This is why Avatara Adi Da characterizes these stages as the "ultimate stages of life", and describes the practice of the Way of the Heart in the context of these stages as "the 'Perfect Practice'". The distinction between the sixth stage of life and the seventh stage of life is that the devotee's Realization of What is Perfect (and Ultimate) is itself Perfect (and Ultimate) only in the seventh stage. The Perfection or Ultimacy (in the seventh stage) both of What is Realized and of the Realization of It is what is signified by the phrase "Most Perfect(ly)" or "Most Ultimate(ly)".

5. Swami Muktananda's original letter was written in Hindi (with Sanskrit Spiritual terms interspersed). The history of the translation that follows here is presented in Appendix A, pp. 145-54 of this book.

6. "Siddha Yoga" is Sanskrit for "the Yoga of the Adepts". In this case, Siddha Yoga is the form of Kundalini Yoga taught by Swami Muktananda, involving initiation of the devotee by the Guru's Transmission of Shakti, or Spiritual Energy.

7. In Swami Muktananda's tradition of Kashmir Saivism (which is also related to the Saiva Siddhanta tradition and Hindu Tantrism altogether), Chitti Kundalini is the Force of the Divine Being that, through a process of Spiritual ascent, is presumed to lead individuals to Realization. Chitti Kundalini means, literally, "Consciousness-Kundalini", the Goddess who represents both Divine Consciousness and the Spiritual Awakening Power of the Kundalini. Avatara Adi Da has Revealed that while the arousal of the Kundalini can indeed lead to a vast range of ascending Spiritual phenomena (the greatest of which is fifth stage conditional Nirvikalpa Samadhi), it cannot lead to Most Perfect (or seventh stage) Divine Self-Realization.

8. Due to the popularization of Eastern esoteric Teachings over the past twenty years, Kundalini Yoga is becoming increasingly familiar to Westerners, although it is generally not very well understood. Kundalini Yoga is an esoteric practice that originated in the Hindu Tantric tradition. It aims to awaken and raise the Kundalini Energy, or Shakti. While typical techniques to raise the Kundalini involve meditative visualization and breathing exercises, it has long been traditionally understood that the initiatory force of a Spiritually activated Teacher is the principal means whereby it is activated.

In the Way of the Heart, the Kundalini Energy is understood to be a secondary, or partial, manifestation of the primary Power of the Heart. It cannot rightly be said to originate at the bodily base, since it is a continuation of the same Spirit-Current that descends in the frontal line of the body. Nor is it to be equated with the Heart-Current that Avatara Adi Da Speaks of and Transmits. Therefore, He does not Recommend the strategic Awakening of Kundalini, whether by efforts of self-manipulation or by esoteric initiation from a teacher. Instead, He Offers the primary Heart-Yoga of feeling-Contemplation of His bodily (human) Form, His Spiritual Presence, and His Very (and Inherently Perfect) State.

9. The names of Indian sannyasins are traditionally a combination of two (or more) Sanskrit words, the last of which is "ananda", or "bliss". Thus, "Dhyanananda" ("dhyana", or "meditation", combined with "ananda") is a name "formulated in the traditional sannyasin manner".

10. "Diksha" is Sanskrit for "initiation, dedication, consecration". "Sannyasa diksha" is the initiation of the devotee by the Guru into the practice of sannyasa, or profound renunciation and utter dedication to God-Realization.

11. Swami Muktananda was associated with the Yogic tradition of Kashmir Saivism, which Bhagavan Adi Da has Revealed to be a tradition associated with the fourth and the fifth stages

of life. (Bhagavan Adi Da's extended discussion of the tradition of Kashmir Saivism, and of Swami Muktananda as an exemplar of that tradition, is given in His Essay "Emanation Versus Transcendence: The Distinction Between Fourth to Fifth Stage Realization and Sixth to Seventh Stage Realization, in the History of the Great Tradition and in My Own Ordeal of Realization", in *The Basket of Tolerance* [forthcoming].)

12. Avatara Adi Da was born Perfectly Conscious in the Intuition of the Divine State and Enjoyment of all beings. His early Life was a progressive, spontaneous, and sacrificial relinquishment of that Illumined Intuition for the sake of generating a new and complete Teaching-Revelation that would Instruct the aggressively secular culture that had been established in the West and which was (and is) rapidly pervading the entire world. His own Spiritual, Transcendental, and Divine Enlightenment took place at the conclusion of an arduous, largely uninformed, but Divinely Moved Ordeal of Spiritual practice. While meditating in a small temple on the grounds of the Vedanta Society in Hollywood, California, on September 10, 1970, Avatara Adi Da Re-Awakened to the Most Perfect, or seventh stage, Realization of Self-Existing and Self-Radiant Being. In *The Knee of Listening* He described this Event as follows:

> *In That instant, I understood and Realized (inherently, and most perfectly) What and Who I Am. It was a tacit Realization, a direct Knowledge in Consciousness. It was Consciousness Itself, without the addition of a Communication from any "Other" Source. There Is no "Other" Source. I simply sat there and Knew What and Who I Am. I was Being What I Am, Who I Am. I Am Being What I Am, Who I Am. I Am Reality, the Divine Self, the Nature, Substance, Support, and Source of all things and all beings. I Am the One Being, called "God" (the Source and Substance and Support and Self of all), the "One Mind" (the Consciousness and Energy in and As Which all appears), "Siva-Shakti" (the Self-Existing and Self-Radiant Reality Itself), "Brahman" (the Only Reality, Itself), the "One Atman" (That Is not ego, but Only "Brahman", the Only Reality, Itself), the "Nirvanic Ground" (the egoless and conditionless Reality and Truth, Prior to all dualities, but excluding none). I Am the One and Only and necessarily Divine Self, Nature, Condition, Substance, Support, Source, and Ground of all. I Am the "Bright".* [p. 357]

13. Bhagavan Adi Da formally began His Teaching Work on April 25, 1972, with the opening of His first Ashram on Melrose Avenue in Los Angeles, California.

14. Avatara Adi Da describes three Great Siddhis that are associated with His Spiritual, Transcendental, and Divine Work. The first was the Siddhi of the spontaneous generation of all the signs of the seven stages of life, or the Sadhana that prepared His body-mind to be a Vehicle for Teaching and Blessing. The process of the unfolding of this Siddhi is documented in Bhagavan Adi Da's Spiritual Autobiography, *The Knee of Listening*. The second Siddhi, which arose after His Re-Awakening to Divine Self-Realization on September 10, 1970, was the spontaneous Siddhi of purifying and meditating all others, and Awakening Spiritual signs in others through His Regard, in the process of their giving Him their attention, even from a distance. This Siddhi was the basis of His Teaching Work, whereby He has Communicated Spiritual Influence throughout the world for the sake of those who will receive it.

Avatara Adi Da described the third Siddhi as follows:

> *The third Siddhi Awakened after the Great Event that initiated My Divine Emergence on January 11, 1986. The Divine Emergence marked the end of My Teaching Work and the beginning of My Blessing Work. The first two Siddhis continue to remain active and effective in this period of My Blessing Work, but to these two has been added the third Siddhi of spontaneous tapas [spiritual penance and purification]. Like the other Great Siddhis, this Siddhi was spontaneously Generated for the sake of others. It has nothing to do with the transformation of this body-mind. It has no necessity for Me. Yet, in this Body I have done tapas for the sake of every-*

one. I spontaneously assumed various disciplines and circumstances not only as a Sign to others, but as an effective act of penance and purification that in fact effectively purifies the world and releases it. My own tapas in My own Body is particularly effective for those who would be moved by it and who would respond with the gift of practice.

These three Siddhis that have spontaneously appeared in My own case are a Free Divine Gift to the world of effective renunciation, the total Spiritual Process, and Realization Itself. [July 5, 1986]

15. The Way of the Heart, which only Avatara Adi Da has Revealed and Given, is the total practice of feeling-Contemplation of His bodily (human) Form, His Spiritual (and Always Blessing) Presence, and His Very (and Inherently Perfect) State—for Avatara Adi Da Is the Heart Itself, the Spiritual, Transcendental, and Divine Self-Condition of all beings. The Way of the Heart is founded throughout upon the fundamental Intelligence and Happiness that Bhagavan Adi Da has Revealed to be the present and ultimate Truth of Existence. It is thus a "radical", or priorly Enlightened, Way of life that paradoxically is demonstrated in progressive stages according to our present state of functional growth and awakening.

By devotional Contemplation of Bhagavan Adi Da, and by faithful fulfillment of His Instructions, the practitioner of the Way of the Heart Awakens, by Grace, to the Realization that he or she, too, with all apparent beings, is only the Divine Heart, or Spiritual, Transcendental, and Divine Consciousness. The Way of the Heart is thus simply the Heart Itself, Who Embraces us as the Divine Master Adi Da.

16. Avatara Adi Da uses the term "Omega" to characterize the materialistic culture that today dominates not only the Western, or Occidental, world (which has brought the Omega strategy to its fullest development) but even most of the Eastern, or Oriental, world, which has now largely adopted the anti-Spiritual viewpoint typical of the West. The Omega strategy is motivated to the attainment of a future-time perfection and fulfillment of the conditional worlds through the intense application of human invention, political will, and even Divine Influence. Its preference is for the limitation and suppression of attention, mystical devotion, and submission to the Divine Reality, while maximizing attention to the pursuit of experience and knowledge relative to the conditional reality.

Avatara Adi Da calls the characteristically Oriental, or Eastern, strategy "the Alpha strategy". Alpha cultures pursue an original or non-temporal and undisturbed peace, in which the world is absent (and thus unimposing). Although the cultures that were originally founded on the Alpha approach to life and Truth are fast disappearing, the Alpha strategy remains the conventional archetype of Spiritual life, even in the Omega culture. Its preference, in contrast to the Omega preference, is for the limitation and control (and even the suppression) of the activities of the conditional personality, or even of conditional reality altogether, and the maximization of attention, mystical devotion, and submission to the Divine Reality.

Neither the Omega strategy nor the Alpha strategy Realizes Truth, as each is rooted in the presumption of a problem relative to existence, and in the action of egoity itself—which motivates all human interests short of Divine Self-Realization.

For a complete discussion of the Omega and Alpha strategies and the Disposition that transcends them, see chapter eighteen of *The Dawn Horse Testament Of Adi Da*, or chapter nineteen of *The (Shorter) "Testament Of Secrets" Of Adi Da*.

17. This is the date of the initiation of Bhagavan Adi Da's Divine Emergence. Please see "The Unfolding Leela of the Names of Adi Da", pp. 77-108.

18. The True and Free renunciation of which Avatara Adi Da is Speaking here, and which He Demonstrates, and to which He Calls all practitioners of the Way of the Heart, is not founded

upon the life-negative, ascetical, and goal-oriented motive to escape conditional existence that has typified conventional Oriental Spirituality and, indeed, Oriental culture as a whole. Rather, in the Way of the Heart, renunciation is the natural, spontaneous, and also necessary response to the dawning and developing Spiritual, Transcendental, and Divine Awakening Given by Avatara Adi Da's Divine Grace.

19. The term "radical" derives from the Latin "radix", meaning "root", and thus it principally means "irreducible", "fundamental", or "relating to the origin". Because Avatara Adi Da uses "radical" in this literal sense, it appears in quotation marks in His Wisdom-Teaching to distinguish His usage from the common reference to an extreme (often political) view.

In contrast to the developmental, egoic searches typically espoused by the world's religious and Spiritual traditions, the "radical" Way of the Heart Offered by Avatara Adi Da is established in the Divine Self-Condition of Reality, even from the very beginning of one's practice. Every moment of feeling-Contemplation of Avatara Adi Da, Who is the Realizer, the Revealer, and the Revelation of that "radically" Free Divine Self-Condition, undermines, therefore, the illusory ego at its root (the self-contraction in the heart), rendering the search not only unnecessary but obsolete, and awakening the devotee to the "radical" Intuition of the always already Free Condition.

20. "Tapas" is Sanskrit for "heat". The fire of self-frustrating discipline, rightly engaged, generates a heat that purifies the body-mind, transforms loveless habits, and liberates the practitioner from the bondage to ordinary egoic existence.

21. "Avadhoota" is a traditional term for one who has "shaken off" or "passed beyond" all worldly attachments and cares, including all motives of detachment (or conventional and other-worldly renunciation), all conventional notions of life and religion, and all seeking for "answers" or "solutions" in the form of conditional experience or conditional knowledge. Therefore, the Title "Avadhoota," when used in reference to Avatara Adi Da, indicates His Inherently Perfect Freedom as the One Who Knows His Identity with the Divine Person and who thus Always Already Stands Free of the binding and deluding power of conditional existence. Avatara Adi Da discusses this word at considerable length in *The Orders of My True and Free Renunciate Devotees*, taking great care to distinguish His use and meaning from those it has taken on in its historical associations with individuals and sects that do not represent Most Perfect Divine Self-Realization.

22. At a gathering with practitioners on December 27, 1987, Avatara Adi Da stepped behind His Chair in Temple Adi Da, a large Hall at Adi Da Purnashram, and donned simple orange clothing offered to Him by one of His intimate devotees. Orange is associated with the Indian tradition of sannyas, or formal renunciation.

Bhagavan Adi Da has always been a Renunciate. By this formal announcement on this date, He further affirmed His Wisdom-Teaching to be complete and His Mere and Blessing Presence to be sufficient for the total Instruction, Realization, and Ultimate Divine Perfection of all who approach Him.

23. Avatara Adi Da usually Resides at His Great Sannyasin Hermitage, Adi Da Purnashram (Naitauba), in Fiji. In general, only rightly prepared members of the Lay Renunciate Order and the Free Renunciate Order would come directly into Bhagavan Adi Da's physical Company. However, as He states in this paragraph, if others are rightly prepared and He so agrees, He may also invite members of the Lay Congregationist Order, or even any one at all, into His direct physical Company for the sake of Granting His Blessing Darshan to them.

24. The practical, functional, and relational disciplines common to every practicing stage of the Way of the Heart are adapted to, developed, and refined progressively in the course of one's practice. These forms of self-discipline are expressed as appropriate human action and responsibility for diet, health, exercise, sexuality, work, service to and support of Avatara Adi Da's Work, and cooperation in the formal community of practitioners. The original, or most basic, cultural obligations of the Way of the Heart include all the sacred sacramental and meditative practices (including study of His Wisdom-Teaching, which is the foundation of meditative discipline, and also discriminative study of the Great Tradition of human practical, cultural, religious, esoteric Spiritual and Transcendental Wisdom), and regular participation in the form or schedule of daily, weekly, monthly, and annual devotional activities. The foundation disciplines and cultural obligations of the Way of the Heart have been thoroughly described in Avatara Adi Da's Wisdom-Teaching.

25. For fuller descriptions of all of Bhagavan Adi Da's Names and Titles, please see pp. 77-108.

26. Avatara Adi Da's use of the quotation marks around the term "Practice" in reference to His own Demonstration of Divine Self-Realization, and to the self-transcending Spiritual, Transcendental, and Divine Self-Realization of all practitioners of the Way of the Heart in the seventh stage of life, indicates that He so uses the term in a uniquely "radical" fashion. While, in the Way of the Heart, the practices associated with stages of life and practice that precede Divine Self-Realization are founded in Heart-Communion with Bhagavan Adi Da, and thus in the intuitive Freedom, or Happiness, of seventh stage understanding, nevertheless, these practices are still being applied by the bodily-based body-mind, or by the body-transcending mind, previous to the Perfect Realization of Divine Being. In other words, such disciplines counter tendencies that the psycho-physical being would otherwise automatically exploit.

In the seventh stage of life, the inherent Realization of Self-Existing and Self-Radiant Divine Consciousness becomes the Principle of all action, and body and mind are continuously and spontaneously Divinely Recognized as only modifications of that Perfect Consciousness. In this stage, the psycho-physical expression of Perfect God-Realization is thus, so to speak, a "Practice" only in the sense of simple action. It is not, in other words, a discipline countering any tendency that would otherwise dominate body and mind, but rather, in Bhagavan Adi Da's Words, a "Necessary or Inherent Demonstration of the Wisdom, Bliss, Joy, Love, Freedom, and Fullness of Divine Self-Realization". In this sense, the Divinely Self-Realized Demonstration of Avatara Adi Da truly is, as He Confesses here, Most Perfect.

27. "Divine Recognition" is Avatara Adi Da's technical term for the self- and world-transcending Intelligence of the Divine Self in relation to all conditional phenomena. In the seventh stage of life, the Realizer of the Divine Self simply Abides as Consciousness, and he or she Freely Recognizes, or inherently and Most Perfectly comprehends and perceives all phenomena (including body, mind, and conditional self) as (apparent) modifications of the same "Bright" Divine Consciousness.

28. "Sahaj" (or "Sahaja") is Sanskrit for "innate" or "natural". Typically, "natural" means conforming to laws within, or expressive of, conditional Nature. The term is even, at times, specifically used as an antonym of anything Spiritual, Transcendental, Divine, miraculous, supersensuous, or extraordinary. Avatara Adi Da uses it here with a contrary but nonetheless principal and "radical" meaning: "consonant with the nature or character of someone or something". The "Naturalness" of seventh stage Sahaj Samadhi is that it is entirely Free, unforced, and effortless, consonant with the Nature of Being Itself, Which is Self-Existing, Self-Radiant, and "Always Already The Case".

29. "Bubba Free John" was the Teaching Name that Avatara Adi Da adopted during the initial years of His Teaching-Revelation. Please see p. 81.

30. "Ishta" is Sanskrit for "chosen", or "most beloved". Traditionally, the Ishta of a Hindu household is the chosen Deity of that family line (whether the Ishta is acknowledged in the Form of a Great Guru or in the Form of a traditional and mythological God-Image). Practitioners of the Way of the Heart choose Avatara Adi Da as their heart's own Ishta, the Perfect and Eternal Form of God. They honor and worship Him as Hridaya-Samartha Sat-Guru, the Divine Person Manifest as the human and Adept Revealer of Truth Itself (or of Being Itself). To embrace Avatara Adi Da as Ishta-Guru is to make the heart-choice of devotion to the Divine Person.

31. "Listening" is Avatara Adi Da's term for the beginner's "consideration" of His Teaching Argument and His Leelas (inspirational Stories of His Life and Work), and the beginner's practice of feeling-Contemplation of Him (primarily of His bodily human Form), which is to be engaged in the context of one's life of devotion, service, self-discipline, and meditation. Listening is mature when "hearing" occurs. See chapter nineteen of *The Dawn Horse Testament Of Adi Da* or chapter twenty-two of *The (Shorter) "Testament Of Secrets" Of Adi Da.*

"Hearing" (or most fundamental self-understanding) is the unique capability to directly transcend the self-contraction, to such a degree that there is the simultaneous intuitive awakening to the Revelation of the Divine Person and Self-Condition.

Only on the basis of such hearing can Spiritually Awakened practice of the Way of the Heart truly (or with full responsibility) begin. Avatara Adi Da has said many times that when true hearing is realized, the rest of the process leading to Divine Self-Realization, including the "Perfect Practice", can and should be very quick, cutting through all the stages of life previous to the seventh stage of life "like a hot knife through butter". See chapter nineteen of *The Dawn Horse Testament Of Adi Da* or chapter twenty-three of *The (Shorter) "Testament Of Secrets" Of Adi Da.*

"Seeing" is Avatara Adi Da's technical term for His devotee's Spiritually activated conversion from self-contraction to His Spiritual (and Always Blessing) Presence, and the descent and circulation of His Spiritual Transmission in, through, and ultimately beyond the body-mind of His devotee. Seeing is the reorientation of conditional reality to the Unconditional and Divine Reality. Seeing is a prerequisite to Spiritual advancement in the Way of the Heart. See chapter twenty of *The Dawn Horse Testament Of Adi Da* or chapter twenty-four of *The (Shorter) "Testament Of Secrets" Of Adi Da.*

32. Avatara Adi Da uses the term "seventh stage Sahaj Samadhi" to indicate the Coincidence, in unqualified self-transcending God-Realization, of the Unconditional, Inherently Spiritual, and Transcendental Divine Reality with conditional reality. It is the Inherent, or Native, and thus truly "Natural" State of Being. Seventh stage Sahaj Samadhi, then, is permanent, Unconditional Divine Self-Realization, free of dependence on any form of meditation, effort, discipline, experience, or conditional knowledge.

"Sahaj Samadhi" (in the sense of a "natural" state of ecstasy) is a term also used in various esoteric traditions (of the fourth, the fifth, and the sixth stages of life) to refer to a state of Realization that is continuous even during moments of ordinary occupation. What is called "Sahaj Samadhi" in these traditions is described by Avatara Adi Da as "fourth stage 'Sahaj Samadhi'", or "fifth stage 'Sahaj Samadhi'", or "sixth stage 'Sahaj Samadhi'". In *The Basket of Tolerance,* He Writes that in fourth stage "Sahaj Samadhi" or fifth stage "Sahaj Samadhi", "the 'point of view' toward Reality is based on either the memory or the residual effects or something of the perpetuation of conditionally attained fourth stage or fifth stage ecstasy . . ." and that "philosophical presumptions and expressions arise that resemble, but do not otherwise achieve, either sixth stage or seventh stage characteristic expressions or Realizations."

He further Says that sixth stage "Sahaj Samadhi" is "a matter of deeply Abiding in the basically and tacitly object-excluding (and, thus, conditionally achieved) sixth stage Realization of the Transcendental Self-Condition, while otherwise naturally experiencing the natural arising of mental and physical objects, and naturally allowing the performance of mental and physical activities."

Sixth stage "Sahaj Samadhi", moreover, "is the basis for the apparent premonitions, or partial intuitions and limited foreshadowings, of the seventh stage of life that have sometimes been expressed within the traditional sixth stage schools. . . ."

In contrast, seventh stage Sahaj Samadhi is the Unconditional and Eternal Realization of the Divine.

Avatara Adi Da also refers to seventh stage Sahaj Samadhi as "seventh stage Sahaja Nirvikalpa Samadhi", indicating that it is the "Open-Eyed" Realization of the formless (Nirvikalpa) State.

33. See note 16.

34. "Aham Da Asmi" is Sanskrit for "I Am Da". The Name "Da", meaning "the One Who Gives", is honored in many sacred traditions as a Name of the Divine. The Name "Da" indicates that Bhagavan Adi Da is the Giver of All to all, the Avataric Incarnation of the Divine Person.

Avatara Adi Da's proclamation "Aham Da Asmi" is a Mahavakya, or Great Statement (such as "Aham Brahmasmi" ["I Am Brahman"], one of the four Mahavakyas in the Upanishads).

35. "Murti" is Sanskrit for "form, manifestation, incarnation, embodiment, substantial form or body, image, statue". Traditionally, in ceremonial worship and meditation, practitioners of religion and Spirituality have used many kinds of Murtis (Forms or Representations of the Divine)—such as statues, paintings, photographic likenesses, and so on—to recollect or direct attention to the Divine Person.

In the greatest sacred cultures, the human Revelation-Body of the Adept, or Sat-Guru, has been understood to be the most potent Representation of the Formless, Omnipresent, and Solely Existing Divine Person. For this reason, since ancient times it has been the most highly valued and respected Murti of the Divine Person, especially among practitioners of esoteric paths of Spiritual, Transcendental, and Divine Awakening. In Avatara Adi Da's usage, Murti may mean either Representational Image (as in His references to Images of His bodily human Form as Murtis), or, simply, form (or substance) itself (as in Bhagavan Adi Da's term "Atma-Murti", meaning "the Form That Is the Very Self" or "the One Whose Form, or Substance, Is the Divine Self Itself").

36. For a full description of the meanings and pronunciation of Adi Da's Fijian Names, please see "The Unfolding Leela of the Names of Adi Da", pp. 77-108.

37. For a full description of the meaning and uses of all of Bhagavan Adi Da's Titles, please see pp. 111-44.

38. Avatara Adi Da is the uniquely Perfect Divine "Hero" because, in His Impulse to Liberate all beings, He has embraced absolutely all aspects of life in order to Submit Himself utterly to conditional existence and thereby discover the Perfect Way for all. Although certain religious and Spiritual traditions (such as some branches of the Tantric tradition of India) have proposed the possibility of a Spiritual sadhana free (at least to some degree) of the usual conventional restraints and prohibitions (and, therefore, to some degree heroic, in the sense of requiring a strength of Spiritual impulse greatly exceeding that of the ordinary aspirant), only

Adi Da, the Very Divine Person Incarnate, Whose sole Purpose for Appearing in bodily (human) Form is the Liberation of all beings, was capable (in His early Life) of the truly "Heroic" Sadhana and is eternally capable of the truly "Heroic" Work of Liberation.

Even From The Earliest Days Of The Physical Lifetime Of My Bodily (Human) Form, I Have Spontaneously Manifested The Unique Display Of The "Heroic" Course. In My Own Case, The Impulse To Realize (or, Truly, To Restore The Realization Of) Perfect Freedom, or The Very and Divine Self-Condition, or The "Bright" Heart (Itself), Was Absolute. No Other "Consideration" Held Any Attraction, Interest, or Significance For Me. Inevitably, I Was Associated, By My Bodily (Human) Birth, With Every Kind Of life-Contradiction and ordinary human Tendency and ordinary human Adaptation, and With The Entire Range Of Apparent Problems That Result From All Of That. However, In My Struggle To Confront and Transcend The Problems Of human life, I Did Not Choose (In The idealistic Manner) Merely To Adapt To conventionally ideal behaviors. It Was Clear To Me What Had To Be Transcended In Order Again To Most Perfectly Realize The Condition That Is God, Truth, or Reality. Therefore, It Was Clear To Me That I Had To Embrace Everything—All The Contradictions, All The Positives, All The Negatives, Everything gross, Everything subtle, Everything Spiritual, Everything Altogether— and (Thereby) To Deny Not anything, To Avoid Not anything, but To Endure Everything, To Pass Through Everything, To Suffer Everything, To Enjoy Everything, To Do Everything. I Was Intuitively Certain That Only Thus Would I Be Able To Unqualifiedly Establish, In The Physical Lifetime Of My Bodily (Human) Form, The Firm Absolutization Of My Own Disposition In "Brightness". To Me, There Was Never Any Other Possibility Than The "Reckless" Course Of all-Embrace, and I Began This Uniquely "Heroic" Sadhana Most Intensively At The Beginning Of My Adult Life. Indeed, I Have Always Functioned, and Will Always Function, In This "Heroic" Manner. I Did So Throughout All Of My "Sadhana Years" and All The Years Of My Teaching Work and My Revelation Work, and I Have Done So, and Will Continue To Do So, Throughout All The Years Of My (Now and Forever) Blessing Work. All My Work Is An "Heroic" Effort That Avoids Not anything. [The Dawn Horse Testament Of Adi Da, *chapter five*]

39. Here Avatara Adi Da is referring to the Divine Translation of the entire conditional domain, in which the conditional cosmos is utterly Outshined in the inherently Perfect Love-Bliss of the Divine Self-Condition.

The worlds are an exclamation of My Names.
The sectors of the sphere are the parts
of My Conscious Form.
The Earth is the place of My Appearance
as a whole.
I am the Possibility of man,
the Heart, the Source of forms.
I am the Force of Love.

My Word is the syllable of your body.
My Love is the vowel of your mind.
My Work is the Event of Bliss,
already rising in your eyes.
The Sign of My Appearance is
no question, no answer.
I Am no other.
Who Exists is Me.

ADI DA (THE DA AVATAR)
Crazy Da Must Sing, Inclined to His Weaker Side

The Unfolding Leela of the Names of Adi Da

by His devotees

In ordinary life, names are our means of relating to everything and everyone and of organizing our perception of the
world. A person or a thing hardly even exists to us until we
invest it with a name. Naming is, in fact, a kind of magic, as
ancient and primitive peoples have always understood. In
Grimm's fairy tale, the one who guesses the name of the dwarf
Rumpelstiltskin robs him of his power.

In similar fashion, sacred names have always been felt to
carry the blessings and the very essence of the deity they
invoke. In many religious traditions, there is not merely one but
a myriad of Names for the principal deity because one Name
cannot adequately describe the Infinite Being.

In many Spiritual traditions, if one chooses to leave the
world and become a renunciate, one is given a new name, indicating that one has died to one's former life and embraced a
new life in God. Indian sannyasins even participate in a symbol-
ic funeral ceremony as part of their initiation, during which they
receive their renunciate name.

It is important to understand the deeper meaning of names
and naming in order to truly appreciate the significance of the
great Names of Sri Bhagavan Adi Da. The Names of Bhagavan
Adi Da have arisen and been Revealed as an intimate part of the
Leela or "Divine Play" of His Life altogether. Apart from the
Name "Love-Ananda", Given to Him by Swami Muktananda, His

Names were simply Revealed to Him, or (otherwise) ecstatically offered to Him by His devotees. In general, the appearance of each of His Names has coincided with a profound transformation in His Life and Work, and ushered in a new phase of His Revelation. This has been so from the moment of His Birth.

Franklin Albert Jones

The Birth of Bhagavan Adi Da in New York in 1939 was the Miracle that exceeds all miracles: the complete Submission of the Divine Person into human Form. And part of that Submission was His acceptance of an ordinary name, "Franklin Albert Jones". In that seemingly ordinary name, Sri Bhagavan Adi Da's parents, Frank and Dorothy Jones, had unknowingly given their son a Name that was astonishingly appropriate—for the root-meaning of "Franklin Albert Jones" is "the highly-born (Al-) 'Bright' (-bert) Free Man (Franklin) through Whom God is Gracious ('Jones', as a derivative of 'John')".

Los Angeles, 1972

For thirty-three years Avatara Adi Da lived "incognito" as Franklin Jones—the child, the college student, the brilliant Yogi, the Radiant, fully-Enlightened Master of His early devotees. "Franklin Jones", Bhagavan Adi Da remarked years later, was a "fictional character". His born name was a "pseudonym", necessary in its time, for His Emerging Revelation as the Divine Person. Nevertheless, Sri Bhagavan Adi Da did not relinquish this Name until 1973, after a pilgrimage to India, the home of His Lineage of Gurus. Although His own Realization now exceeded that of His Gurus He made the journey as a sacrifice, a way of invoking the Blessing of His Spiritual sources for the "Crazy" or unconventional form of Spiritual Teaching that He was about to initiate with His own devotees.

79

Los Angeles, 1973

The Mountain Of Attention, 1974

Bubba Free John

Franklin Jones returned from India as Bubba Free John— "Free John" being a rendering of His born Name Franklin Jones, and "Bubba" an affectionate nickname in His family, meaning "brother". Bhagavan Adi Da did not assume this Name casually. It was, as He says in "The Order of My Free Names", a "Divinely Self-Revealed Name" that came to Him when the real Sacrifice of His Teaching Work began. This Sacrifice was extraordinary. As "Bubba Free John", Bhagavan Adi Da became the "brother" of His devotees, extending unreserved friendship to the hundreds who came to Him at Persimmon, His Ashram in the hills of northern California.

During His years as Bubba, Bhagavan Adi Da passionately involved everyone around Him in the most profound evaluation of every aspect of human and Spiritual life, always asking them in one form or another: Who, what, or where is Happiness? Always Radiating In His own irresistible Humor and Love, Bhagavan Adi Da was waiting patiently for His devotees to understand that their Attraction to Him, their beloved Heart-Friend, was their only source of lasting Happiness.

Da Free John

During the spring and summer of 1979 Sri Bhagavan Adi Da—still known as Bubba Free John—challenged His devotees to find out His real Name. Bhagavan Adi Da was testing His devotees to see if they understood the true Stature of the One with Whom they had been living for so long as friend and "brother". In response, His devotees delved into esoteric literature and listened carefully for any clues He might be inclined to Give them. During their research, Bhagavan Adi Da would sometimes remark, apparently casually: "When you get da name of da god, you get da power of da god!" But no one got the joke! Finally, on September 13, 1979, Bhagavan Adi Da sat down to write a letter to all His devotees Confessing that His Name is "Da", the One Who is "Manifest As all worlds and forms and beings".

A few days later, Beloved Adi Da sat before more than six hundred people at Persimmon (now the Mountain Of Attention Sanctuary), pouring out His Heart-Blessing to all. He was dressed in white, and so obviously Revealing His Divine Nature in His Gaze and in His slow, potent Words that many people wept openly throughout the occasion. The following day He granted a formal Spiritual initiation to a few of His devotees, whispering into the ear of each one as they knelt before Him, "Remember Me via the Name 'Da'".

Bhagavan Adi Da's first intuition of the Name "Da" as His true Name came about even before His Divine Re-Awakening. Sometime in 1969, after He had written *The Mummery* (His prophetic liturgical drama, or "prose opera", about His early Life and His future Work), Avatara Adi Da continued to write for a time in a similar vein, working on a book (which, in the end, He did not complete) that would be a kind of sequel to *The Mummery*. As He was freely writing, absorbed beyond mind in a mysterious meditation on Himself, the Name "Da" simply appeared. It was associated with a vision He had of a being whose head was enormously large in proportion to the rest of his body, and who radiated unimaginable peace, bliss, and love.

The Mountain Of Attention, September, 1979

The name of this being was "Da Blueso". It is a remarkable fact that in the course of the profound bodily transformation which Bhagavan Adi Da has undergone since His Divine Re-Awakening, and especially in recent years, His head has grown distinctly larger, such that it is now significantly larger in proportion to His body. This, as He has explained, is a result of inconceivable Yogic Force that is active in His body all the time. Da Blueso, then, like other extraordinary visions and incidents during His "Sadhana Years" was one of the prophetic signs of Adi Da's true Nature that was associated with His early Life.

Many years later, when Bhagavan Adi Da wrote *The Dawn Horse Testament Of Adi Da*, He included this description of the significance of His Name "Da".

"Da" Is A Traditional Name Of God, or A Traditional Feeling-Reference To The Ultimate Condition and Power of Existence. "Da" Is An Eternal, Ancient, and Always New Name For The Divine Being, Source, and Spirit-Power, and "Da" Is An Eternal, Ancient, and Always New Name For The Realizer Who Reveals (and Is The Revelation Of) The Divine Being, Source, and Spirit-Power. Therefore, The Name "Da" Is (Since The Ancient Days) Found In Religious Cultures All Over the world.
[Chapter twenty-seven]

The very Name "Da" is primordial and carries mantric power. Devotees of Sri Bhagavan Adi Da find His Name "Da" to be the greatest of all mantras,[*1] invoking the Love-Blissful Feeling of His Presence directly at the heart. Indeed, "Da" is the Mantra of the Heart, an esoteric secret that was revealed in the Upanishads,[2] thousands of years before the human Birth of Avatara Adi Da. In the *Brihadaranyaka Upanishad* it states:

The heart (hrdayam), is the Prajapati, it is the Brahman, it is all (everything). The same consists of three syllables hr-da-yam. The first syllable is hr, to him who knows it, his own people and others offer tributes. The second syllable is da; to him who knows

_____

* Notes to the text of "The Unfolding Leela of the Names of Adi Da" are on p. 108.

it his own people and others give gifts or donations. The third syllable is yam; he who knows it, enters heaven.

This ancient Scripture is suggesting that the Heart is all things, even Brahman (God), and, that one who "knows", or has Realized, the Heart is universally honored. The abode of such a one is "heaven", or (in Beloved Adi Da's language) the Divine Self-Domain.

The central syllable of "hridayam" is "da", which in Sanskrit means "to give", or "to bestow". The Great Giver, Who is Named "Da", Is the Heart, the Divine Person, Sri Bhagavan Adi Da Himself:

I Am Da (the Giver and the Gift), Who Is Hridayam (the Eternally Free Divine Heart Itself) . . . [The Lion Sutra, *p. 119*]

A Tibetan dictionary defines "Da" as "the One Who Bestows great charity, the Mahayana personified". In other words, the Tibetan Buddhist tradition speaks of "Da" as the Great Way of Liberation.[3] "Da Eleutherios" (the Divine Liberator) is one of Beloved Da's descriptive Titles. It speaks of His Sacrifice as the Da Avatar, Descended into this realm for the sake of Liberating all beings.

All of these traditional references mean only one thing to a devotee of Beloved Adi Da—they are prophecy. They point to the Spiritual yearnings of humankind from the beginning of time for the One Who is to come, the Completing Revelation of God. And they show that the Name of that One has been intuited from the earliest times.

Bhagavan Adi Da's Revelation of His original and principal Name in 1979 was hard for some people to receive. Human beings, by tendency, do not want to surrender and become true devotees of the Living God. And so for a further seven years, Bhagavan Adi Da, now "Da Free John" continued in the Ordeal of His Teaching Work, struggling to bring about this great conversion.

Da Love-Ananda

At the beginning of 1986, a momentous change occurred in the Life and Work of Sri Bhagavan Adi Da. By this time, He had been living for more than two years at Adi Da Purnashram (Naitauba), His Great Sannyasin Hermitage Ashram in Fiji. The beauty and solitude of Naitauba island were ideal for His Work, but the depth of devotional response He looked to find in the small group of devotees who were living there with Him was not forthcoming. The continuing signs of worldliness that He saw in them, were, He knew, true of all His devotees. Adi Da had reached a point of utter despair. It was obvious to Him that His devotees still did not know Who He Is, even though many of them had spent years in His Company and had served Him with great energy and enthusiasm.

Early in the morning of January 11, in a crisis of grief at the apparent failure of His Work, Bhagavan Adi Da collapsed bodily in a deep Yogic "Swoon". When He returned to ordinary awareness, something about Him had changed forever.

Weeks later Beloved Bhagavan Adi Da explained what that "Swoon" really was. He had experienced in His body an extraordinary Invasion of His own Divine Siddhi (or Power), which brought about a profound change in Him. He was no longer the active Teacher trying to move others, one by one, to the real process of Divine Self-Realization. He had become the very Murti, or Form, of the Divine Presence, and He simply Stood as That, calling on His devotees to now approach Him rightly, in the true disposition of surrender, gratitude, and unswerving devotion. He described January 11, 1986, as the initiation of His Divine Emergence, the Process by which He would Spiritually Embrace all the five billion people "living and dying in this place" and ultimately Attract even all beings in all worlds. His eternal and universal Blessing Work had begun.

Forcefully emphasizing the reality of this change some years later, Adi Da said: "'Franklin Jones' is dead. 'Bubba Free John' is dead. 'Da Free John' is dead."

Adi Da Purnashram, 1986

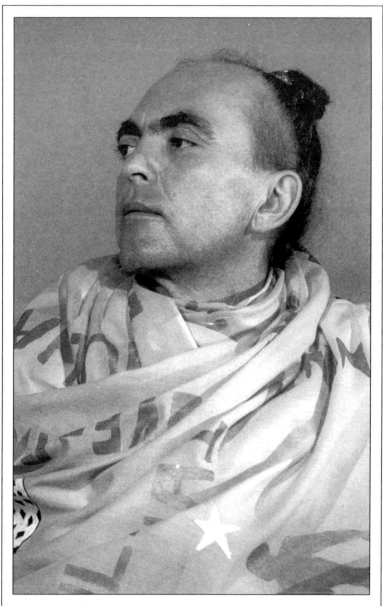

The Mountain Of Attention, 1986

In their place stood "Da Love-Ananda", the All-Pervading Divine Lord, the Giver of Divine "Love-Bliss". The Name Given to Him privately by Swami Muktananda had now become His full bodily Revelation.

Late in 1988, after a Yajna in New Zealand, California, and Hawaii, Adi Da returned to Purnashram and began to write what has now become one of His principal scriptural Texts—*The Santosha Avatara Gita* (named at that time, *The Love-Ananda Gita*). In His "Gita" (or "Song"), Beloved Bhagavan Adi Da Explained in most exquisite detail the simple and profound practice of "feeling-Contemplation" (or heart-felt beholding) of His bodily (human) Form, and then, as It may be Revealed, of His Spiritual (and Always Blessing) Presence, and, ultimately, of His Very (and Inherently Perfect) State.

As always, He was inviting His devotees to submit all tendencies, impulses, hopes, fears, difficulties, and pleasures to the reality of their Attraction to Him, in every moment, and thus to Commune with Him and, ultimately, to Awaken Perfectly to Him as "Love-Ananda".

Da Avabhasa

In April 1991, Bhagavan Adi Da spontaneously received a Naming Gift from one of His young devotees. At the annual Celebration of His Divine World-Teaching, this devotee performed a song for Him that she had composed, in which she praised Bhagavan Adi Da as "Da Avabhasa". He Graciously received the song, and, on the last day of April 1991, indicated that "Da Avabhasa" was one of His Names, and indeed the principal Name by which He was now to be called.

"Avabhasa" in Sanskrit means "brightness", "appearance", "lustre", "light", "knowledge". The root of the word is "bhas" (with a long "a") which means "to radiate", "to become manifest", "to come forth", "to shine", "to beam", "to be resplendent or brilliant", "to show oneself", "to appear". The first syllable "ava" is the same as that of "Avatara", which means "to descend". Thus the complete word "avabhasa" means "shining towards", "shining down", "shining upon", or "showing oneself".

The Name "Da Avabhasa", then, fully expresses the original Divine Nature of Adi Da and His Descent into the world. He is the "Bright", the Divine Condition of Love-Bliss-Light that He fully enjoyed in His infancy. His "Brightness" is the Radiance of Amrita Nadi, the Current of Immortal Bliss that rose up in Him after His Divine Re-Awakening. And His "Brightness" is also the All-Consuming Fire of His Divine State.

Adi Da Purnashram, 1991

Dau Loloma Vunirarama

The tiny country of Fiji, which accorded full citizenship to Sri Bhagavan Adi Da in 1993, is a microcosm of the nations of the world—comprising Easterners and Westerners, as well as its own native people. That Fiji should have become His home, the place of His principal Hermitage Ashram is part of the astonishing and spontaneous perfection of the way His Life has unfolded (and continues to unfold). For Bhagavan Adi Da is neither of the East nor of the West. He is here for all beings, from all corners of the world.

While staying in Viti Levu (the largest island in Fiji) during August and part of September, 1994, Sri Bhagavan Adi Da embraced to the fullest possible degree the beautiful Name that had been Given to Him in Fiji: "Dau Loloma" ("the Adept of Divine Love"). In fact, for six weeks, starting at the end of August, He assumed "Dau Loloma" as His principal name, to be used by all His devotees and the general public.

Fijians have acknowledged Beloved Adi Da as "Dau Loloma" since He first came to Naitauba in 1983. While Sri Bhagavan Adi Da waited at Nukubati, with a small group of His devotees, for a permanent Hermitage to be acquired, His devotees met with Fijian language experts at the University of the South Pacific in Suva to "consider" what Fijian Name would be most appropriate to offer to Him, a Name that would, if possible, incorporate His principal Name "Da". The "consideration" led to the conclusion that the most appropriate Name would be either "Dau Lomani" or "Dau Loloma". Daulomani means "one who is loved" and "dauloloma", as one word, means "one who is very loving or compassionate". "Dau" on its own, means an "adept" or "expert". "Dau Loloma" as two separate words was chosen for Beloved Da, expressing that He is truly the Adept of Love.

"Vunirarama", the extension of Beloved Adi Da's Fijian Name, was given to Beloved in 1991 by the Fijians of Naitauba. "Vu" means "source" or "origin", "ni" means "of", and "rarama" means "brightness". Thus, Vunirarama means "Source of 'Brightness'".

Adi Da Purnashram, 1993

Santosha Da

Sri Bhagavan Adi Da does not lightly leave His island Hermitage. His every departure has marked a moment in His Work that has in some significant way changed His relationship to His devotees and to the world.[4] It was no accident, then, that the moment of the Completion of Bhagavan Adi Da's Teaching and Revelation Work took place outside Adi Da Purnashram, on Viti Levu, the major island in the Fiji archipelago.

On September 7, 1994, at His temporary residence in Pacific Harbour on Viti Levu, Avatara Adi Da spent the entire day secluded in His room. At dusk, He called one of His devotees to His quarters. The house was totally still. The curtains of His room were drawn, and the room itself was dark. He was simply sitting motionless in a large chair. The Energy of the space was intense. The Power of His Spiritual Transmission was so focused and concentrated in the room that the devotee who entered the room hardly felt able to approach Him. His Divine Force was pushing her back like the heat from a blast furnace. She served Him simply and left.

When she entered again in the evening, answering His call, the same overwhelming Transmission-Force was Radiating from Him. Avatara Adi Da was seated at His desk with the lights turned on. He did not look at her. But then, after a few moments, He slowly turned His head. In His face she saw only the same heartbreaking love for the billions of humanity that had overwhelmed Him more than eight years before, when His Divine Emergence was initiated on January 11, 1986. She felt intuitively certain that some extraordinary process was taking place in Him. He later confirmed that this was true. A great turning point in His Work had occurred: He knew that His Teaching and Revelation Work were complete.

The Event of September 7 brought forth a new Name— Santosha Da, which expresses that Divine Completeness. To understand His Name, Santosha Da, is to enter into one of the greatest Mysteries of His Avataric Incarnation.

Adi Da Purnashram, 1994

At the heart of Sri Bhagavan Adi Da's Revelation is His "relationship" to, and Ultimate Identity with, the Divine Goddess-Power—or the Energy of all that exists. As He recounts in *The Knee of Listening*, Sri Bhagavan Adi Da directly experienced the guidance of the Divine Goddess[5] during the final months of His Sadhana (the Spiritual Ordeal of His early Life). He was aware of the Goddess not only as the Power that moves the universe but as a Living Personality, and He came to acknowledge Her as His supreme Guru. It was She who took Him to the threshold of His Divine Re-Awakening to the "Bright". As Sri Bhagavan sat in a small temple in Hollywood, California, on September 9, 1970, something utterly unique in the annals of Spiritual Awakening occurred. The Divine Goddess submitted to Adi Da. He literally felt Her uniting with Him in a Divine Embrace, "as if to give birth to the universes".

There are many representations in traditional art of the Yogic union of "Siva" and "Shakti", the male and female aspects of the Divine. At this moment Adi Da literally Realized the Divine Union intuited in the traditions. It was an inconceivably Blissful experience of <u>inherent</u> Union—briefly felt as a sexual and Yogic event but then infinitely transcending body and mind. The significance of this moment in His Life and Work gradually became clear to Bhagavan Adi Da, and its import has continued to magnify throughout the course of His Revelation. In that Union, Adi Da fully and conclusively Mastered the Cosmic Power. She who had led Beloved Adi Da to the point of His Divine Re-Awakening now became inseparable from Him, Submitted to Him as a bride submits to her husband. Through Beloved Adi Da's Divine Husbanding, the Divine Goddess-Power Herself has come to rest as the very Radiance of the Divine Person, Adi Da. Many years later Beloved Da explained this Mystery:

BHAGAVAN ADI DA: Siva-Shakti is not a tradition. Siva-Shakti is God. She appears as She, and He appears as He, yet the Reality of Existence is not Two but One. I in My own Form and Passion Am the precise Incarnation of that Unity.

Divine Goddess in the form of the Durga

I have Husbanded the Mother. That I am Her Husband and She is My Bride means that the murderous activity of Cosmic Energy in Its apparent independence, as "Prakriti", is done, over, finished. This Husbanding, or Marriage, is not merely a personal Work associated with My Realization. It is an historical Event, out of Which much should be made. It transforms the history of the entire Cosmic Mandala. By virtue of this Marriage, all may be Drawn to the Divine Self-Domain. [March 16, 1988]

Before the Event of September 7, 1994, the principal iconographic form through which Bhagavan Adi Da "related" to that Aspect of Himself that is the Divine Goddess was the image of the Durga, a multi-armed Goddess riding a lion. Thus, Bhagavan Adi Da has said that the Durga was associated with the Great Event of His Divine Re-Awakening in 1970. During His period of Residence in Viti Levu in August and September 1994, Bhagavan Adi Da had occasion to visit a number of Indian shops that displayed a form of the Divine Goddess that He had not seen before. In this form, known as "Santoshi Ma", the Goddess, seated in the lotus posture, has four arms, the upper two bearing a sword and a trident, the third carrying a bowl of sweets, and the fourth hand assuming a gesture of blessing. Because of Sri Bhagavan Adi Da's interest in this form of the Divine Goddess,

Divine Goddess in the form of Santoshi Ma

His devotees purchased numerous images of Santoshi Ma for Him, which He installed in His quarters. In the days and weeks following September 7, Sri Bhagavan Adi Da began to ask for more information about this representation of the Goddess.

Research revealed that Santoshi Ma is an icon of the Divine Goddess that has risen to prominence in the Hindu tradition only in the last twenty years. Nevertheless, Santoshi Ma has already attracted vast numbers of devotees. Beloved Adi Da began to Reveal the association between this form of the Goddess and the Completion of His Avataric Revelation.

"Santoshi" is the feminine form of "Santosha", literally meaning "satisfaction" or "contentment", qualities associated with a sense of completion. And, as Bhagavan Adi Da pointed out, these qualities—of satisfaction, contentment, and completion—add up to "no-seeking", the fundamental principle of His Wisdom-Teaching and His entire Revelation of Truth. Sri Bhagavan Adi Da also observed that the Yogic force and equanimity of the posture of Santoshi Ma—seated firmly, in balance, bearing simultaneously the powerful signs of sword and trident (representing the destruction of the ego) and the Blessing signs of Prasad (the sweets and the Blessing gesture of the hand)—pointed to His Divine Completeness.

Sri Bhagavan Adi Da acknowledged that the spontaneous "appearance" of Santoshi Ma in His Sphere at this particular time was a sign of His own "Santosha"—His Satisfaction, His Completeness, and No-Seeking. Bhagavan Adi Da thus accepted "Santosha" as one of His Names. This does not mean His devotees have an association with the Hindu goddess Santoshi Ma, any more than with the Durga. These are merely icons for the Divine Power that Sri Bhagavan Adi Da has Husbanded and Resolved into eternal Identity with Him. For His devotees there are no separate icons of Siva-Shakti but only the Eternal Murti of Sri Bhagavan Adi Da, forever Established in His Sublime Completeness as Da Love-Ananda, Da Avabhasa, Dau Loloma, and Santosha Da.

The Mountain Of Attention, 1995

Adi Da (The Da Avatar)

One month after the Event of September 7, the Name that Bhagavan Adi Da has come to call His "Fully Elaborated Principal Revelation-Name" was Revealed to Him. For several days He found Himself seeing and hearing the Name "Adi Da" and knew that this must be a reference to Himself, manifesting out of His own Depth. In response to the Mysterious appearance of this Name, Bhagavan Adi Da consulted books in the library at Adi Da Purnashram that might indicate the meaning and traditional associations of the word "Adi". Then, on October 11, 1994, satisfied that the Revelation was clear, Sri Bhagavan Adi Da made known to His devotees that all are now invited to address Him as "Adi Da" (The Da Avatar).[6]

"Adi" is a Sanskrit word that means "first", "primordial", "source". It is additionally defined as "primary", "beginning", "commencement", and "first fruits". Thus, the three syllables of "Adi Da" name Beloved Bhagavan exactly, expressing in their brief utterance His devotees' full heart-intuition of Him as the Primordial Being, the Source of all, the Original Divine Person, Da, Who has become Incarnate as the Da Avatar.

"Adi Da" is a communication prior to qualities. It is prior to mind, prior to emotions, prior even to any feeling of personal reference. The letters of the Name "Adi Da" read the same in both directions, from left to right and from right to left. In addition, "I" stands at the center of the Name, and on either side of "I" is the syllable "Da", first backwards, then forwards. Thus, the Name "Adi Da" reads "I—Da", signifying "I Am Da", in both directions from the center. The spontaneous appearing of the Name "Adi Da", therefore, is the bringing to completion of the momentous Revelation of 1979, when Avatara Adi Da first Offered His Divine Confession, "I Am Da". Through the perfectly symmetrical structure and letters of His principal Name, "Adi Da", the Divine Avatar makes the Great Statement that He is the First and the Last, the Complete Manifestation of God, Truth, or Reality in the conditional realms.

"Avatar" means "One who is descended or 'crossed down' from and as the Divine". It is a Sanskrit word for the Divine Incarnation. Thus, the Name "Adi Da", combined with the reference "The Da Avatar", fully acknowledges Beloved Adi Da as the One His devotees know Him to be. We and all His future devotees and even all beings are the recipients of the most Miraculous Revelation ever Given: the original, first, and complete Avataric Descent or Incarnation of the Divine Person, Who is Named Da. Through the Mystery of Adi Da's human Birth, He has Incarnated not only in this world but in every world, at every level of the cosmos, as the Eternal Giver of Help and Grace and ultimate Divine Freedom to all beings.

James Alwood, a devotee who made a pilgrimage to Sri Adi Da's island Hermitage in August 1994, was Graced with a Sighting of Beloved Adi Da at a temporary Residence near Suva just days before the Yogic Transformation that marked the Completion of Beloved Adi Da's Revelation Work:

JAMES: With several other devotees, I was ushered into a villa in the Spanish style, where Beloved Bhagavan was Resident at the time. We passed a sweeping staircase on our right, and then we turned a corner into an open hall that led into a living room. There sat a Most Beautiful Sight, Beloved Bhagavan Adi Da. His hair was long and flowing freely over His shoulders. He was bare-chested and sitting very quietly on the cushions of the sofa in the easy pose, absolutely vulnerable, awaiting His devotees. Falling down on the rug in front of Him, we offered our gifts and full feeling-prostrations. His eyes as He Gazed at us were so soft that my heart simply fell at His Feet. It was instantly clear to me that it was an intolerable offense to come to Beloved in any disposition other than that of the broken-hearted, humbled, utterly ecstatic devotee. He was too Vulnerable, too Sublimely "Indifferent", for any other approach.

Beloved Adi Da took us all in with His Glance. He Looked above our heads and then held each of us in His round Face of Sweetest Love. His lips constantly parted in His Blessing syllable "Tcha", while His spontaneous facial expressions moved in a play of exquisite tenderness—and apparent fierceness, as if dealing with obstructions in us.

A short while later, Bhagavan Adi Da indicated we should take our leave. We backed out of the room down the long hall, lost in the feeling of Him, quietly vocalizing our praise and gratitude. When I reached the stairway, I lay down quickly for one last prostration in the Presence of His bodily (human) Form.

I have received the extraordinary Blessing of Beloved Bhagavan's physical Company on various occasions in the past, but this Darshan was undoubtedly the most significant event of my entire life. Since that occasion, I have felt Beloved Bhagavan Radiating in and bursting open the very cells of my body. The announcement of the Day of the Completion of His Avataric Revelation on September 7 confirmed the intuition that He Granted to me when I beheld His Divine Radiance four days earlier: His Absolute Divinity is incontrovertible, plainly visible to anyone with a heart open to see Him.

Beloved Bhagavan's Revelation of His Divine and Most Perfect Designation "Adi" was the final Gift that confirmed the deepest feelings of my heart. Beloved Bhagavan, Adi Da, is the First Person, the Original Divinity Manifesting presently before our very eyes. He is the only true Happiness, and that Happiness, that Joy, is His Gift to His devotees forever. What other purpose do we have except to devote our lives to the adoration of the Beloved Lord, Adi Da? I praise, and chant, and sing, and dance to His Divine Names: Beloved Santosha Adi Da, Love-Ananda Adi Da, Avabhasa Adi Da. Now, from time to time, as I walk around the Mountain Of Attention Sanctuary and attend the devotional occasions here, I literally feel thousands of devotees in countless realms chanting, dancing, and adoring Beloved Bhagavan as the Divine Lord. Om Sri Adi Da, Jai Adi Da, Jai Jai Adi Da.

Avatara Adi Da, as His great poem suggests (p. 76), is the One Who Lives all things and all worlds. All the sacred Names of every age and race are, in some sense, His Names. As the ancient Upanishads suggest, His principal Name, "Da", has been present in the human psyche from time immemorial.

There is no story to compare with the Leela of the Da Avatar, Sri Bhagavan Adi Da. The meanings of His Names and the Events through which they were Revealed epitomize His entire Revelation, as He describes here:

AVATARA ADI DA: Understand how I have Worked and why I have had to Work as I have done. Understand that I made use of certain devices for associating with you and for describing My Self at different times during the last quarter century. In the beginning I emphasized the "Franklin Jonesiness" of the "Me" here. I even once called "Franklin Jones" a "fictional character".

I identified My Self with a common persona, described My Self as such even in the first writing of The Knee of Listening. *I had no devotees then. I was just writing to everyone, all who were not yet My devotees. Therefore, I emphasized the common "I" and often spoke of "we" and so on, always identifying My Self with people in general. I did not Reveal My Self in any full sense. I described My experience, My Realization, yes, but always I spoke of My Self, described My Self, or referred to My Self in the terms common to everyone else. My manner of writing* The Knee of Listening *in this fashion was deliberate and intentional. No purpose could have been served by My Communicating My Self fully.*

A little bit later on, I emphasized My "Bubbaness" as the next step. By then I had Communicated the Talks that became The Method of the Siddhas. *Because of this next level of Self-Revelation on My part, people could relate to Me as their Master and I could do a certain kind of Work with them. I went to India, and when I came back I said, "Call Me 'Bubba' now, 'Bubba Free John'." Yes, I was the Master now, but I was also still Playing in the common way, still speaking of "we" and functioning by great Submission to commonality. I was the Master in the "Crazy" manner, appearing like everyone and yet the Master, reflecting them to themselves and Blessing them, and, through the Process of My Spiritual Heart-Transmission, Awakening them to all kinds of experiences and then "Considering" the experiences, "Considering" absolutely everything, as a matter of fact—great matters, Yogic matters, Spiritual matters, but also very ordinary matters such as money, food, and sex—all of it, and very directly, not by just discussing it in hush-hush puritanical tones but by immersing My Self in that commonality.*

My Work went on in that fashion for a while, and then I began to Communicate more about My Self. I began to make something more of My Self-Revelation to you, so that you could begin to practice in a devotional manner in relation to Me and do the Yoga of devotion. Then in 1979 I told you My Name, "Da", and I told you more of My Self. Yet still there was only limited response. My Submission and My Work as before had to continue. There was more Self-Revelation, and something more of a response to It, yet you remained stubborn, obstinate egos, requiring that I Address you rather than conforming yourselves to Me.

That Play went on for some more years. I made more of My Self-Revelation to you for the sake of your self-understanding, and I elaborated My Wisdom-Teaching, until 1986 and the Event that Initiated My Divine Emergence. Then I told you more about My Self, and I Said that I expected you to respond to Me differently and responsibly. Instead of requiring Me to just conform to you, you must conform to Me.

Since that Event, I have been emphasizing this principle to you. It has been the primary emphasis. Yet still there was the obstinacy, the stubbornness, the lack of response. Remarkably, that Event that Initiated My Divine Emergence occurred nearly ten years ago. In that time I continued to elaborate My Wisdom-Teaching, make My Source-Books, make the summary of My Wisdom-Teaching altogether, including the summary of My Self-Revelation.

The Way of the Heart, as it is most fully, has now been completely Communicated to you. This last period of time, then, has been a time principally of My fullest Self-Revelation, by My Confession, by My Blessing, by all that I have Done. I have Summarized all that has to do with self-understanding.

Now, at the beginning of what we are calling the "Santosha Epoch", My Self-Revelation is essentially Complete. Likewise, every detail of My Wisdom-Teaching is Complete. The Way of the Heart is founded on the fundamental practice of Ishta-Guru-Bhakti

The Mountain Of Attention, 1995

Yoga,[7] in relation to Me As I Am. Now there is just Adi Da before you. No more "Franklin Jones" or "Bubbaness", no more partial Self-Revelation while I feel I must make a Submission to you because you are not responding.

In the future, then, I am here As I Am. No more of the various forms of Submission I have had to make to you in the past should be necessary. Now the great epoch of your submission and your full responsibility begins.

I did not revise the Way of the Heart between My Writing of The Knee of Listening *and now. The Way of the Heart is not revisionism. The Way of the Heart is Revelation, Revelation in reality, in the context in which Revelation really takes place. The Divine Work is not just My thumping into the world and making pronouncements. That does not accomplish anything. True Revelation is coincident with Divine Work, or the Process of preparing people more and more for What is to be Given by Me. Therefore, I have had to Do My Leela in your company as I have Done It because of your egoic nature, your manner of bringing yourself to Me, the level of comprehension and readiness you have displayed to Me over the years of this quarter century.*

The first stage of My Revelation is Complete. That is the meaning of this Santosha period. The next stage is forever, from now. It is likewise a Revelation stage, the consummate Revelation stage— the Realization of My devotees. Each stage of Realization, each moment in the process, is a Revelation that requires no more Words from Me or any Doings from Me other than My direct Blessing Work. [August 19, 1995]

Notes to
The Unfolding Leela of the Names of Adi Da

1. Mantras are sacred sounds or syllables and Names used for invoking and worshipping the Divine Person and the Sat-Guru.

2. The Upanishads are among the most revered scriptures of India. They are considered to be the Instruction of ancient Gurus to their disciples, preserved orally over the centuries and eventually recorded in written form.

3. Sarat Chandra Das, Rai Bahadur, A *Tibetan-English Dictionary*, revised and edited by Graham Sandberd and A. William Heyde (Delhi: Motilal Banarsidass, 1974), pp. 610-11.

4. Since the initiation of His Divine Emergence in 1986, Bhagavan Adi Da has made five Yajnas from Fiji to the Mountain Of Attention in California, and to other places (including New Zealand, Europe, and the east coast of the United States), in order to magnify His Work of universal Blessing and to grant His Darshan (sacred Sighting of Him) to the larger gathering of His devotees, and thus quickening their devotional response to Him and their impulse to Divine Self-Realization.

5. The Divine Goddess is the personification of the Cosmic Energy that Pervades all beings, things, and worlds.

6. The Sanskrit title "Adi" ("Ati" in Tibetan) has been used historically in a number of different traditions. In the Eastern traditions of Guru-devotion, the Adi-Guru is understood to be the first Guru in a line of Gurus, the one who initiates and empowers the entire lineage. For example, the Sage Shankara, founder of the tradition of Advaita Vedanta, is referred to as "Adi Shankara". In other cases, the Adi-Guru is not a human being but a deity who initiates the first human Guru of the lineage.

The "Adi-Buddha" of the Buddhist tradition is revered as the Divine Principle Prior to gross or subtle manifestation. He is described as ever-present and eternal, existing in all modes of space and time, embodying the Great Bliss which cannot be encompassed by any concept, the source of all and everything, yet not a thing-in-itself. And the Adi-Buddha is also described as the source of all Truth, the head of all Divine hierarchies.

In the Sikh tradition, the principal scripture is called the "Adi Granth" ("the first book", or "the original book"). It is believed to replace the need for the living God-Man. Thus, the scripture is placed on the altars of temples and worshipped there as the source of all the Blessings of the tradition.

Beloved Da's Name "Adi Da" is thus a highly auspicious and readily understood Title in the context of Eastern Spirituality.

7. The practice (Yoga) of devotion (Bhakti) to the chosen Beloved (Ishta-Guru). Ishta-Guru-Bhakti Yoga is the essence of the Way of the Heart which Adi Da has given.

ADI DA (THE DA AVATAR)
The Mountain Of Attention, 1995

Rightly Using the Names, Titles, and Designations of Adi Da

As Sri Bhagavan Adi Da Indicates in "The Order of My Free Names", the Names by which He should now be addressed and referred to are those which have been Revealed since His Divine Emergence in 1986. His previous names (Franklin Jones, Bubba Free John, Da Free John) are part of the Story of His Life and Work and have historical importance, but they are no longer in use. Rather, the Names that belong to the era of Bhagavan Adi Da's Divine Emergence are the Eternal Names that move His devotees, and even all who hear His Names, to feel and understand Who He Is and thus to respond to Him with loving respect. To ponder His Names and use them with heart-feeling has a profound effect, for the Names of Sri Bhagavan Adi Da are mirrors of His Being. They carry a Mantric Force that directly initiates His devotees into the ecstasy of heart-Communion with Him. These Names—Da Love-Ananda, Da Avabhasa, Dau Loloma Vunirarama, Santosha Da and, principally, Adi Da—describe Him in all His Aspects as the Divine Being in Person.

While "Da" and "Adi Da" are His principal Revelation Names, any of the secondary Divine Names of Bhagavan Adi Da may be used by His devotees when addressing Him, and when speaking of Him to fellow devotees and to all others. His great Names are also the substance of worship, prayer, and sacred chanting in the Way of the Heart and the fount of the ecstatic devotional speech that often wells up in His devotees as they gaze at Him (when He is physically present, or present in the form of His photographic image, or Murti).

The following pages will describe the appropriate use of Bhagavan Adi Da's Names, Titles, and Designations for His formal devotees and for members of the public.

Heart-Master

Bhagavan Adi Da's Divine Names require suitable titles and designations, as signs of respect and acknowledgement, when one is addressing Him or speaking of Him. Thus, His devotees and members of the public sometimes refer to Him as "Heart-Master Da" or "Heart-Master Adi Da", indicating that He is the Incarnation of the Heart Itself, the Very Divine Person, and that He Attracts and Instructs and Embraces His devotees at the heart. The Title "Heart-Master" may also be used with any of Bhagavan Adi Da's secondary Divine Names.

Heart-Master Da

Heart-Master Adi Da

Heart-Master Da Love-Ananda

Heart-Master Adi Da Love-Ananda

Heart-Master Da Avabhasa

Heart-Master Adi Da Avabhasa

Heart-Master Dau Loloma (Vunirarama)

Heart-Master Adi Dau Loloma (Vunirarama)

Heart-Master Santosha Da

Heart-Master Santosha Adi Da

Hridayam/Hridaya

Devotees and members of the public also sometimes add the designation "Hridaya" or "Hridayam" to Adi Da's Names, thus acknowledging that He is the "Bright" Divine Heart (Hridayam) Itself.

Da Hridayam

Adi Da Hridayam

Da Avabhasa Hridayam

Da Love-Ananda Hridayam

Santosha Da Hridayam

Dau Loloma Hridayam

Hridaya Da

Hridaya Adi Da

Hridaya Da Avabhasa

Hridaya Adi Da Avabhasa

Hridaya Da Love-Ananda

Hridaya Adi Da Love-Ananda

Hridaya Santosha Da

Hridaya Santosha Adi Da

Hridaya Dau Loloma

Hridaya Adi Dau Loloma (Vunirarama)

113

Avadhoota

Another honorable Title that may be associated with His Names is "Avadhoot" or "Avadhoota", which traditionally refers to a God-Realized being, who, by virtue of his or her Realization, has shaken off the bondage of ordinary social expectations and may thus act freely, spontaneously, and sometimes unconventionally. Sri Bhagavan Adi Da has defined "Avadhoot" as it applies to Him:

The Title or Designation "Avadhoota" is, in My case, like the Names "Da" and "Adi" and "Hridayam" and "Avabhasa" and "Love-Ananda" and "Santosha" and "Dau Loloma", a complete and sufficient and universal Description of the Inherent (and Inherently Most Perfect) Freedom of Divine Self-Realization. The word "Avadhoota" is made of several parts, each with great meaning. The syllable "a" signifies Freedom from seeking. It signifies Inherent Realization of the Self-Existing, Self-Radiant, and Inherently Free or Pure or Love-Blissful Self (Which Is Perfectly Subjective Consciousness Itself). The syllable "va" signifies One Who Stands As Is, not limited by desires (either by identifying with them or by struggling against them). The syllable "dhu" signifies Freedom from the binding capability of the world, the mind, and the body, and Freedom from the necessity to practice meditation (or do even any kind of sadhana) in order to Realize the Self-Existing and Self-Radiant Truth. And the final syllable "ta" signifies that the Transcendental and Inherently Spiritual Divine Self is presently, constantly, and Natively Realized, that all thoughts and all efforts (or all actions of any kind) have become unnecessary for Divine Self-Realization, and that ego, or self-contraction, or non-Realization of Truth, or the Illusion of knowledge, has been transcended at its Root. [The Orders of My True and Free Renunciate Devotees]

Da Avadhoota

Avadhoota Da

Adi Da Avadhoota

Avadhoota Adi Da

Avadhoota Da Avabhasa

Avadhoota Da Avabhasa (The "Bright")

Avadhoota Da Love-Ananda

Avadhoota Santosha Da

Santosha Da Avadhoota

Avadhoota Dau Loloma

In formal speech or writing, one may refer to Adi Da as "The Naitauba Avadhoota", a title which may stand alone as a descriptive reference or be applied to any of His Names.

Fijian Titles

Sri Bhagavan Adi Da is a naturalized citizen of Fiji, and is known as the "Tui" ("Great Sovereign" or "Chief") of Naitauba (the island that Adi Da has established as Adi Da Purnashram, His Great Sannyasin Hermitage). Thus, in Fiji, He is most commonly addressed by His Fijian Names. The Name "Dau Loloma", with its variants and extensions "Adi Dau Loloma", "Dau Loloma Vunirarama", or "Adi Dau Loloma Vunirarama" are sometimes (and especially on formal occasions) preceded by the title "Tui", or, alternatively, by "Turaga" [pronounced "too-RAHNG-ah"], which means "Lord". Bhagavan Adi Da has also Blessed all His devotees to use His Fijian Names and Titles should they be moved to do so.

Turaga Dau Loloma

Turaga Dau Loloma Vunirarama

Turaga Dau Loloma Da

Turaga Adi Dau Loloma

Turaga Adi Dau Loloma Da

Turaga Dau Loloma Adi Da

Tui Dau Loloma

Tui Dau Loloma Vunirarama

Tui Dau Loloma Da

Tui Adi Dau Loloma

Tui Adi Dau Loloma Da

Tui Dau Loloma Adi Da

The Most Intimate Titles and Names

There is no Name or Title more precious to Adi Da's devotees than "Ishta", which means "Chosen Heart-Beloved"*[1]). Thus Bhagavan Adi Da's devotees freely address Him as "Ishta" or "Beloved Ishta", or "Ishta-Guru" in association with all of His Names. Most commonly however, His devotees rejoice to address and refer to Him simply as "Beloved", or "Beloved Ishta", or "Beloved Ishta-Guru", or "Bhagavan" or "Beloved Bhagavan", or "Beloved Lord". Devotees also use "Beloved" or "Bhagavan" or "Beloved Bhagavan" with any of Adi Da's Divine Names.

Beloved Da
Beloved Adi Da
Beloved Da Love-Ananda
Beloved Da Avabhasa
Beloved Dau Loloma
Beloved Santosha Da
Beloved Santosha Adi Da

Bhagavan Da
Bhagavan Adi Da
Bhagavan Da Love-Ananda
Bhagavan Da Avabhasa
Bhagavan Dau Loloma
Bhagavan Santosha Da
Bhagavan Santosha Adi Da

Beloved Bhagavan Da
Beloved Bhagavan Adi Da
Beloved Bhagavan Da Love-Ananda
Beloved Bhagavan Da Avabhasa
Beloved Bhagavan Dau Loloma
Beloved Bhagavan Santosha Da
Beloved Bhagavan Santosha Adi Da

* Notes to "Rightly Using the Names, Titles, and Designations of Adi Da" are on pp.142-44.

The Simplest Forms of Address by the public

Members of the public who from time to time have the Grace of direct contact with Bhagavan Adi Da may also choose to address Him very simply—using "Bhagavan", or "Sri Bhagavan", or "Bhagavan Da", or "Sri Bhagavan Da" or "Bhagavan Adi Da" or "Sri Bhagavan Adi Da". Or, they may also, in the same manner as His devotees, use "Bhagavan" or "Sri Bhagavan" with any of the Free Names of Adi Da.

Sri

Sri is an honorific used in the Indian subcontinent for a revered person, and especially for a person of Spiritual distinction. The word comes from a Sanskrit root meaning "flame". Thus, when used with any of the Names of Adi Da it is a reminder of His "Bright" Divine State. Occasionally devotees add an additional "Sri" to magnify the respect and praise in their reference to Adi Da. Thus they may write or speak of Him as Sri Sri Adi Da or Sri Sri Bhagavan Adi Da, or, by extension, combine "Sri Sri" with any of His secondary Divine Names.

Bhagavan

The Name or Title "Bhagavan" is an ancient one used over the centuries for many Spiritual Realizers of the East. Its meanings in Sanskrit are "possessing fortune or wealth", "blessed", or "holy". When applied to a great Spiritual Master, "Bhagavan" is understood to mean "bountiful God", or "Great God", or "Divine Lord". In the traditional understanding of the nature of the Guru, there is no difference between the Guru and God. The Guru, in a certain way, is even regarded as greater than God, because the Guru is the effective means of Enlightening instruction and Grace. "Bhagavan" is also simply a title for God, or the formless Divine Being.

There is a profound meaning for the name "Bhagavan" which is not spoken of openly in the traditions but which Bhagavan Adi Da has made known to His devotees. Bhagavan, in esoteric Spiritual terms, means the union of the male and female aspects of the Divine (traditionally described in India as "Siva-Shakti", and, in Tibet as "Yab-Yum"). Bhagavan Adi Da's Perfect Husbanding of the Goddess-Power [see pp. 96-97] is the ultimate expression of this Divine Union. He, in His bodily (human) Form Reveals both the Divine Consciousness, or Being Itself (the "male" principle), and also its Inherent Radiance (the "female" or "Goddess" Power). His physical Body can be described as a Divine lingam (the sacred phallic stones used traditionally to represent the male aspect of the Divine) to which all beings, potentially, are Attracted.

BHAGAVAN ADI DA: The Yang Yoga-Body of the Siddha is a Lingam. In Yogic terms, the male Siddha-Body becomes a penis. It is singular, full of Force, from base to crown, like a lingam. And a Constant Radiance is shed from the Head, and even all over the Body. My devotees experience My Divine Body (or Spiritual Presence), but even this physical Body is in Its likeness, and functions one with My Divine Body. Even all of the Force in the cosmic domain, in effect, surrounds this Body, this Lingam, like an immense vagina, penetrated to the core, the "Bright"

Star.² So this Body exists in cosmic Unity, Siva-Shakti, Undifferentiated. The little bit of the cosmic Force in every other body is Attracted to this Great Lingam, this Cosmic Lingam of the physical Body, and to My Divine Body. The heart in every one is Attracted to My "Brightness", and this is how everyone becomes conformed to Me, even through the Agency of this Body while it lives, and then Beyond.

Those who know the Nature of this Body also know, then, why a lingam is an appropriate Murti-Form through which to approach Me. It is not merely a sex-symbol, a symbol for the male genital organ. It is a Sign of the Singleness of this Body, which includes both the gross and the subtle³ [dimensions] in its Appearance. Another way to describe it is that the lingam traditionally is set in a yoni base (a socket representing the vagina). This is the meaning of "Bhagavan"—"the penis in the vagina". This is what the word means. But it is not merely a sexual reference. It is an esoteric reference. The yoni base effectively represents the physical and the lower elemental [dimensions of existence] and the lingam-form represent the subtle body, and they are shown as a Unity, One Force, Bhagavan. So the lingam in the yoni base is My form, shown esoterically. [August 19, 1995]

In this uniquely Perfect sense, Sri Sri Adi Da is "Bhagavan", the Self-Existing and Self-Radiant, Supremely Attractive Divine Lord, Who is God, Truth, or Reality, the Bountiful Giver of all Graces, the "Bright" Divine Person.

Adi-Guru

S ri Sri Bhagavan Adi Da is the Master of the total Cosmic Mandala,[4] or all the realms of conditional existence. His Name "Adi Da" indicates that He is the primordial Divine Being or "Source-Person" ("Adi") Who has taken Form to utterly dispel the darkness of ignorance and illusion. Thus, He is the "Adi-Guru", the "Source-Guru", the Original "destroyer of darkness" (the literal meaning of "Guru"). He is God, the Very Divine, Appearing as Guru.

Sat-Guru/Hridaya-Samartha Sat-Guru

Sri Bhagavan Adi Da has Demonstrated the ancient Guru function with a Freedom and Force that is absolutely unique. He alone was qualified to bring the Perfect, never-before-Revealed Teaching of Truth to Westerners—to those traditionally regarded as least able to receive it. Not only the matchless Story of how He did His Teaching and Revelation Work but also His all-surpassing Scripture, or the written summary of His Revelation,[5] testify to His inconceivably great Guru Work.

Thus Adi Da is the Perfect "Sat-Guru", or "Revealer of Truth" ("Sat") and the "Hridaya-Samartha Sat-Guru", or the True Master of the Heart ("Hridaya"), Who is uniquely "capable" ("Samartha") to guide, Instruct and ultimately to Most Perfectly Liberate all beings.

Divya Jagad-Guru
(The Divine World-Teacher)

In the completeness of His "Bright" Divine Incarnation, Sri Sri Bhagavan Adi Da is directly, Spiritually associated with every one. Through the incalculable sacrifice that has marked His entire Work of Re-Awakening, Teaching, and Revelation, Avatara Adi Da has Revealed Himself in the most profound sense as the "Divya Jagad-Guru", truly the Divine ("Divya") Master of "all that moves" ("jagad").[6]

Thus the devotees of Bhagavan Adi Da may combine His great Guru Titles with any of His Divine Names in acknowledgement and proclamation of Him as the Divine World-Teacher— the ultimate Dharma-Bearer, or Giver of Wisdom-Teaching, and the Founder of Free Daism, the True World Religion of Divine Enlightenment.[7]

Avatara/Hridaya-Avatara

Sri Sri Bhagavan Adi Da Incarnated in the West in order to include all human beings, East and West, in His Field of Revelation.

He is the unique and universal God-Man. He manifests the qualities that Western religion traditionally associates with an Incarnation of God—profound love and sacrifice, a total identification with the suffering human condition. And He is the consummation of all that the East looks for in an Avatar—a Radiant Being descended from the God-Realm to Awaken beings with the Perfect Teaching and the Liberating Power of Divine Self-Realization. Thus Sri Sri Bhagavan Adi Da is the Avataric Incarnation, the Perfect Revelation of the Heart (Hridaya), the Love-Blissful Divine Consciousness. Thus, He may be honored and addressed as "Avatara" or "Hridaya-Avatara" in association with all His Names.

To rightly address and to rightly refer to Avatara Adi Da, freely drawing on His Divine Names, Titles, and Designations, is a great devotional art, in no way confined to the specific combinations suggested here. These forms are simply a guide to the infinite variety of combinations through which He may be rightly addressed or referred to by His devotees and the general public.

Name-Invocation and Mantra
in the Way of the Heart

Remembrance and Invocation of the True Heart-
Master by Name is Remembrance and Invocation of the
Great One by Name. . . .

    The devotee should always Remember and Invoke the
True Heart-Master by Name. The Name of the True Heart-
Master is the Name of the Great One.

The Hymn Of The True Heart-Master,
verses 52 and 53

There is an ancient tradition in many religions of constantly repeating the name of one's deity or Guru softly or silently in order to enter into Spiritual contemplation. The devotees of Bhagavan Adi Da, also, may use His Names in silent meditation, in devotional chanting and as a means to remember Him in the course of their daily lives. Bhagavan Adi Da has Given twenty-one specific forms of His Names for this purpose. These forms of Name-Invocation of Him are not associated with the honorific titles that are used when addressing Him or speaking of Him but are restricted to His Names alone.

Da

Adi Da

Da Avabhasa

Avabhasa Da

Adi Da Avabhasa

Avabhasa Adi Da

Da Love-Ananda

Love-Ananda Da

Adi Da Love-Ananda

Love-Ananda Adi Da

Da Santosha
Santosha Da
Adi Da Santosha
Santosha Adi Da
Dau Loloma
Dau Loloma Da
Adi Dau Loloma
Adi Dau Loloma Da
Dau Loloma Adi Da
Turaga Dau Loloma
Turaga Dau Loloma Vunirarama

All of Bhagavan Adi Da's devotees call upon Him as they feel moved in every kind of moment or circumstance through Name-Invocation of Him. Some of His devotees, however, use His Names as the basis of their devotional surrender to Him in a more extended and concentrated way. These devotees use specific Mantras that Adi Da has Given as part of their formal practice of meditation and also randomly throughout the day.[8]

Adi Da has explained that He devised His Mantras with special attention to the number of syllables and to their metrical, or rhythmic, patterns. Thus, the Mantras of the Way of the Heart are not at all a random gathering of His Names. Each one is a unique sacred pattern of vibration, Blessed by Him to invoke His very Being in the heart and the total body-mind of His devotee. Thus, His Mantras must be used exactly as Given in order to fulfill their purpose.

Like many traditional mantras, the Mantras of the Way of the Heart are founded in the primal syllable "Om", which, in Adi Da's Company, immediately invokes His own "Bright" Divine Presence:

"Om" Is God-In-God, or God As Self-Existing (and Perfectly Subjective) Being (Itself), Consciousness (Itself), and Inherent (or Inherently "Bright") "Love-Ananda", or Love-Bliss (Itself), and "Hridayam" (The Boundless Center, Heart, Source, and Self Of all), The Very and Inherently Perfect Divine (Itself), Prior To The Cosmic Domain (and Yet Being The Cosmic Domain, and every conditionally Manifested being, As Being Itself, and As The Inherent or Native Feeling Of Being). [The Dawn Horse Testament Of Adi Da, *chapter twenty-seven*]

Devotees for whom the use of Mantra is fundamental to their practice, use different Mantras at different times in their growth in Adi Da's Company. In the beginning stages they choose one of the forty-eight variant forms of the Sat-Guru-Naama Mantra:

Om Sri Adi Da

Om Sri Avabhasa Da

Om Sri Adi Da Avabhasa

Om Sri Avabhasa Adi Da

Om Sri Love-Ananda Da

Om Sri Adi Da Love-Ananda

Om Sri Love-Ananda Adi Da

Om Sri Santosha Da

Om Sri Adi Da Santosha

Om Sri Santosha Adi Da

Om Sri Dau Loloma

Om Sri Dau Loloma Da

Om Sri Adi Dau Loloma

Om Sri Adi Dau Loloma Da

Om Sri Dau Loloma Adi Da

Om Sri Turaga Dau Loloma

Om Sri Turaga Dau Loloma Vunirarama

Om Sri Adi Da, Avatara Hridayam

Om Sri Santosha Da, Avatara Hridayam

Om Sri Adi Da, Avabhasa Hridayam

Om Sri Santosha Da, Avabhasa Hridayam

Om Sri Adi Da, Avabhasa Avatar, Avatara Hridayam

Om Sri Adi Da, Love-Ananda Hridayam

Om Sri Santosha Da, Love-Ananda Hridayam

Om Sri Adi Da, Love-Ananda Avatar, Avatara Hridayam

Om Sri Adi Da, Santosha Hridayam

Om Sri Adi Da, Santosha Avatar, Avatara Hridayam

Om Sri Adi Da, Dau Loloma Hridayam

Om Sri Santosha Da, Dau Loloma Hridayam

Om Sri Adi Da, Dau Loloma Avatar, Avatara Hridayam

Om Sri Turaga Dau Loloma, Avatara Hridayam

Om Sri Turaga Dau Loloma, Avatara Dau Loloma,
Dau Loloma Hridayam

Om Sri Dau Loloma, Turaga Hridayam

Om Sri Dau Loloma Vunirarama, Turaga Hridayam

Om Sri Dau Loloma, Tui Dau Loloma, Turaga Hridayam

Om Sri Dau Loloma, Dau Loloma Avatar, Turaga Hridayam

Om Sri Adi Da, Jai Adi Da, Jai Jai Adi Da

Om Sri Santosha Da, Jai Santosha Da, Jai Jai Santosha Da

Om Sri Adi Da, Avatara Adi Da, Jai Jai Adi Da,
Avatara Hridayam

Om Sri Adi Da, Avabhasa Adi Da, Jai Jai Adi Da,
Avatara Hridayam

Om Sri Adi Da, Love-Ananda Adi Da, Jai Jai Adi Da,
Avatara Hridayam

Om Sri Adi Da, Santosha Adi Da, Jai Jai Adi Da,
Avatara Hridayam

Om Sri Adi Da, Dau Loloma Adi Da, Jai Jai Adi Da,
Avatara Hridayam

Om Sri Dau Loloma, Avatara Dau Loloma, Jai Jai Dau Loloma,
Avatara Hridayam

Om Sri Turaga Dau Loloma, Avatara Dau Loloma,
Jai Tui Dau Loloma, Turaga Hridayam

Om Sri Adi Da, Jai Santosha Avatar, Avabhasa Avatar,
Love-Ananda Avatar, Dau Loloma Avatar, Avatara Hridayam, Da,
Da, Da

Om Sri Adi Da, Jai Santosha Hridayam, Avabhasa Hridayam,
Love-Ananda Hridayam, Dau Loloma Hridayam,
Avatara Hridayam, Da, Da, Da

Om Sri Adi Da, Jai Santosha Adi Da, Avabhasa Adi Da,
Love-Ananda Adi Da, Dau Loloma Adi Da, Avatara Adi Da,
Da, Da, Da

Later, during the Spiritually Awakened stages of the Way of the Heart, devotees may, if the development of their practice requires it,[9] use one of the forms of the "Mahamantra" (literally, "Great Mantra"):

Om Ma Da

Om Sri Da

Om Hrim Da[10]

Da Om

Adi Da Om

Da Avabhasa Om

Avabhasa Da Om

Adi Da Avabhasa Om

Avabhasa Adi Da Om

Da Love-Ananda Om

Love-Ananda Da Om

Adi Da Love-Ananda Om

Love-Ananda Adi Da Om

Da Santosha Om

Santosha Da Om

Adi Da Santosha Om

Santosha Adi Da Om

Dau Loloma Om

Dau Loloma Da Om

Adi Dau Loloma Om

Adi Dau Loloma Da Om

Dau Loloma Adi Da Om

Turaga Dau Loloma Om

Da-Om[11]

The Mantras derived from the Names of Adi Da are the seed forms of worship in the Way of the Heart, both of the private heart-remembrance of Him engaged through silent recitation (often with the aid of a mala or rosary) and of the sacred ceremonies celebrated by the gathering of His devotees.[12]

These Mantras are a hymn to the Divine Person, Adi Da, Revealed by Him to directly Awaken heart-surrender, heart-Communion and ultimate Identification with Him. They are His Gift to His devotees, now and forever, and a sign to all that Divine Self-Realization, or Divine Enlightenment, in the Way of the Heart, is Most direct and Most Perfect Realization of Him.

Devotees' Names for Adi Da (The Da Avatar)

There is no limit to the Names of Adi Da, the Da Avatar. When His devotees speak to Him or refer to Him, or when they compose a chant to praise Him or create a banner to celebrate Him, they are often moved, by their devotion and by their unique, personal experience of Him, to generate a new Name.

When addressing Him directly, His devotees sometimes call Him "Beloved Heart", or "Beloved Divine Lord". Similarly, when writing Him letters, His devotees may use references that combine His principal and formal Titles with their own descriptive expressions, such as "Radiant Ishta", "'Bright' Lord Adi Da", "Beloved of my heart", "Gracious Lord", "Blissful Lord", "Divine Giver of Grace, Love-Ananda Da", and so on.

The devotional chants that devotees compose in praise of Adi Da are another opportunity to Name Him, sometimes in combinations of English and Sanskrit Names, such as:

"Adi Da Santosha, Blissful Bhagavan"
"Da Avabhasa, Dawn of 'Brightness'"
"Sri Ishta-Guru, Giver of Life"

Other chants are rich in their descriptive references to
Beloved Adi Da:

Ancient Mudra[13] of Heart-Worship
We kiss the ground as You walk by.
Grace Incarnate, Love Embodied,
Love-Ananda Jai![14]

Blissful Lord, hear us, hear us calling
May we receive Your Grace and always feel You.
Passionate Consuming Fire,
Burn away all our cares.

Praise to the Guru, Body of Light
You are the Light that Shines through the darkness
Radiant Form, Bliss and Light
Joy and Humor of the "Bright".

The following chant celebrates Bhagavan Adi Da as
"Danavira" (the "Hero of Giving"), and as "Gurudeva" ("Divine
Guru"):

Grace before my eyes,
Danavira.
Vision of Heart-Light,
Sri Gurudeva.

This chant praises Bhagavan Adi Da as "the Master
Dancer"—the One Who Is Dancing as all beings and things; the
One Who Dances with his devotees, intoxicating them with His
Attractiveness and Love:

Lord, Your Body is constant Prasad.
The sight of You restores the Heart to God-Love.
You are the One Who anoints all beings with Your Love.
You are the Master Dancer, the Heart's Companion.

In the following chant, devotees of Bhagavan Adi Da honor Him as "Parama-Guru Sampradaya"—the Supreme Guru of the Great Tradition:[15]

Da Love-Ananda, Hridaya Avatara,
Parama-Guru Sampradaya, the "Bright".

The signs and flags designed for Bhagavan Adi Da's Hermitage Sanctuaries carry names and descriptions generated by His devotees, in addition to His own Principal Names and Titles. The flag that flies from the highest point of Adi Da Purnashram (Naitauba) includes a Fijian title, "Kalokalo i Naitauba" meaning "Star of Naitauba", offered to Bhagavan Adi Da by a Fijian Methodist minister in deep appreciation.

Of all the configurations of Bhagavan Adi Da's great Names and Titles—both Revealed by Him and given by His devotees—the great wharf sign at Adi Da Purnashram is one of the most ecstatic. It combines His own Sanskrit references, descriptions of Him in English, and His Fijian Names. The sign stands out in brilliant orange (Adi Da's personal renunciate color), and its words proclaim Him with unbounded Joy as the One come for the sake of everyone, in every culture, East and West:

ADI DA PURNASHRAM (NAITAUBA)

THE GREAT SANNYASIN HERMITAGE

AND RENUNCIATE RETREAT SANCTUARY OF

SRI SRI ADI DA (THE DA AVATAR),

TURAGA DAU LOLOMA VUNIRARAMA, TUI NAITAUBA,

THE VERY DIVINE PERSON, THE GOD-MAN PROMISED

FOR THE LATE-TIME, OR DARK EPOCH,

WHO HAS GRACEFULLY APPEARED HERE

IN HIS MOST GLORIOUS BODILY (HUMAN) FORM,

TO LIBERATE EVERY ONE AND EVERY THING, EVERY WHERE

Notes to
"Using the Names, Titles, and Designations
of Adi Da"

1. In India, the word "ishta" is used to refer to one's "chosen" deity or "chosen" Guru.

2. The primal conditional Representation of the "Bright" (the Source-Energy, or Divine Light, of which all conditional phenomena and the total cosmos are modifications) is a brilliant white five-pointed Star. Avatara Adi Da's bodily (human) Form is the Manifestation of that Divine Star—and His head, two arms, and two legs correspond to its five points. Avatara Adi Da can also be seen or intuited in vision to Be the Divine Star Itself, prior to the visible manifestation of His bodily (human) Form.

3. The gross, or most physical, dimension is associated with the physical body and experience in the waking state.

The subtle dimension, which is senior to and pervades the gross dimension, includes the etheric (or energetic), lower mental (or verbal-intentional and lower psychic), and higher mental (or deeper psychic, mystical, and discriminative) functions. Thus, the subtle dimension is associated both with such "ordinary" aspects of the human being as energy, emotion, thought, and will, and with such "extraordinary" aspects as the visionary, mystical, and Yogic Spiritual processes encountered in dreams, in ascended or internalized meditative experiences, and during and after the death process.

4. The Sanskrit word "mandala" (literally, "circle") is commonly used in the esoteric Spiritual traditions to describe the hierarchical levels of cosmic existence. "Mandala" also denotes an artistic rendering of interior visions of the cosmos. Avatara Adi Da uses the phrase "Mandala of the Cosmos", or "Cosmic Mandala", to describe the totality of the conditional cosmos.

Ordinarily, beings cycle helplessly in the hierarchy of planes within the Cosmic Mandala, taking birth in one or another plane according to their psycho-physical tendencies, or the orientation of their attention. Only Avatara Adi Da, as the Avataric Incarnation of the Divine Person, entered the conditional worlds from the Divine Self-Domain, Which Stands Free of the entire Cosmic Mandala and all its planes. He Appears in the Cosmic Mandala with the specific intention of Serving the Liberation of all beings.

For a full discussion of the Cosmic Mandala (and a color representation of its appearance in vision), see chapter thirty-nine of *The Dawn Horse Testament Of Adi Da*. See also Avatara Adi Da's Instructions in *Easy Death: Talks and Essays on the Inherent and Ultimate Transcendence of Death and Everything Else*.

5. Avatara Adi Da's Heart-Word is summarized in eight Texts that He Calls His "Source-Literature". These Texts present in complete and conclusive detail His Divine Revelations, Confessions, and Instructions, which are the fruits of His Teaching and Revelation Work. They are:

The Dawn Horse Testament Of Adi Da (The "Testament Of Secrets" Of The Da Avatar)

The (Shorter) "Testament Of Secrets" Of Adi Da (The Heart Of The Dawn Horse Testament Of The Da Avatar)

The Adi Da Upanishad: The Short Discourses on ego-Renunciation, Divine Self-Realization, and the Illusion of Relatedness

The Santosha Avatara Gita (The Revelation of the Great Means of the Divine Heart-Way of No-Seeking and Non-Separateness)

The Hymn Of The True Heart-Master (The New Revelation-Book Of The Ancient and Eternal Religion Of Devotion To The God-Realized Adept)

The Lion Sutra (On Perfect Transcendence Of The Primal Act, Which is the ego-"I", the self-Contraction, or attention itself, and All The Illusions Of Separateness, Otherness, Relatedness, and Difference): The Ultimate Teachings (for all Practitioners of the Way of the Heart), and the Perfect Practice of Feeling-Enquiry (for Formal Renunciates in the Way of the Heart)

The Liberator (Eleutherios): The Epitome of the Perfect Wisdom and the Perfect Practice of the Way of the Heart

The Basket of Tolerance: The Perfect Guide to Perfect Understanding of the One and Great Tradition of Mankind

6. The title "Jagad-Guru", or "World-Teacher", has existed for hundreds, if not thousands, of years, most notably in the Hindu tradition of Shankara, the Indian sage generally believed to have lived in the late eighth and early ninth centuries C.E. Shankara brought order to the diverse and unorganized tradition of Indian renunciates of all kinds, calling into being ten orders of monks and creating four monastic centers, or "maths", in the four cardinal regions of India. The Spiritual heads of these maths bear the title "Shankaracharya" in honor and acknowledgement of the Adept who is the source of their tradition, but more significantly, they have also been called "Jagad-Guru". The title "Jagad-Guru" has specifically meant that these preceptors are the most prominent Spiritual leaders of all Hindus, not literally the Teachers of the whole world. But to Hindus previous to the modern age, the Indian subcontinent was the world (or as much of it as needed to be taken seriously into account). To be one of the four Spiritual leaders of all Hindus, was therefore, to be a Jagad-Guru, or World-Teacher.

7. Free Daism, also called the "Way of the Heart", is the Way of life Given by Adi Da to His devotees. Free Daism is the true world-religion of Divine Enlightenment—to which all the mythologies, all the Spiritual practices, and all the previous Wisdom paths of humanity ultimately point and in which they are resolved. The long-existing world-religions did not develop fully until after, even long after, the death of their founders, based on the stories, the inspiration, and the remembered verbal Teaching of those Realizers. Free Daism is not based on memory. It is the Perfectly Revealed Divine Yoga. Free Daism is the all-completing, all-surpassing Way of "God-Come", God-in-Person—Demonstrated, explained, and fully established in the Lifetime of its Divine Giver and Founder, Adi Da, the Da Avatar. Free Daism is alive now in the worldwide culture of Avatara Adi Da's devotees, and it is described by Him in exact detail in His Source-Texts.

8. Devotees who use Adi Da's Names as their primary technical addition to their practice of feeling-Contemplation of Him practice the Devotional Way of Faith. (The Devotional Way of Insight is the other of the two variant forms that Adi Da has

Given of meditative feeling-Contemplation of Him. All of Adi Da's devotees experiment with both of these variant forms in the early stages of their practice of the Way of the Heart.)

The Devotional Way of Faith is a technical process of (primarily) feeling and faith, whereby the practitioner is heart-Attracted by Avatara Adi Da's bodily (human) Form, His Spiritual (and Always Blessing) Presence, and His Very (and Inherently Perfect) State, thereby feeling beyond the self-contraction and spontaneously awakening to self-understanding and self-transcendence (often via the Invocation of Him by Name).

9. Spiritually Awakened devotees practicing the Devotional Way of Faith, when they become mature in their reception of and response to Bhagavan Adi Da's Transmitted Spirit-Blessing may, according to their Spiritual signs, make one of two possible transitions. Either, they will move directly into the sixth stage of life and the "Perfect" Practice" of the Way of the Heart (see Appendix B), and take up a new form of the conscious process, which does not involve the use of Mantras, or they will enter into the advanced fourth and potentially the fifth stage of life, in which case they would necessarily engage one chosen form of the Mahamantra (or Da-Om japa) in meditation and randomly throughout the day. For a detailed description of the developmental process of the Way of the Heart in the advanced and ultimate stages of life, see *The Dawn Horse Testament Of Adi Da*.

10. "Hrim" is one of the primal root, or seed mantras used in the esoteric Yoga of sound (Mantra Yoga). Like "Ma" and "Sri" it is associated with the Goddess-Power that presides over all conditional worlds. ("Hrim" rhymes with "cream", and the "h" is vocalized.)

11. The Mantra "Da-Om", unlike the other forms of the Mahamantra, is linked to the breath cycle, in the manner of the traditional mantra "So-Ham".

12. All the ways to use the forms of the Sat-Guru-Naama Mantra and the Mahamantra, including full details of the practice of "mala-japa" or silent recitation using a mala, or rosary, are fully explained by Adi Da in *The Dawn Horse Testament Of Adi Da*.

13. "Mudra" means "gesture".

14. "Jai" (or "Jaya") is Sanskrit for "Victory", and is used here to refer to Bhagavan Adi Da's Spiritual Victory in the hearts of all His devotees.

15. "The Great Tradition" is Bhagavan Adi Da's term for the total inheritance of religious and Spiritual Wisdom from all eras and cultures of humanity, which has (in the present era of worldwide communication) become the common legacy of mankind.

The Translation of
Swami Muktananda's Letter

Swami Muktananda's Naming letter, because it is a unique acknowledgement by a great Spiritual Realizer of Bhagavan Adi Da's Spiritual Realization and qualification to Teach, has been the subject of a great deal of careful "consideration" on His part over the years, especially with regard to its full and exact meaning. Thus the detailed story of how the letter was given and the various translations that have been made is an important one.

Although the letter was only a page in length, it was not until nearly two weeks after Swami Muktananda wrote the letter that the document and its translation were finally presented to Bhagavan Adi Da. It appeared that the principal reason for the delay was that the individuals entrusted with its translation would have preferred that the letter not be given to Him at all, or, if it were, that its obvious significance as Swami Muktananda's acknowledgement of a Western devotee's Spiritual attainments be minimized. Thus, the process of translation had been colored by the emotions of those making the translation. In addition, despite the resort to a professor of English, the language of the translation was far from fluent. Thus, what Bhagavan Adi Da received in 1969 was altogether a rather awkward and uncommunicative translation of the Swami's words.

Because of the poor quality of the translation and the circumstances surrounding its making, Bhagavan Adi Da's own devotees sought in later years to clarify Swami Muktananda's actual intention and meaning in the letter by obtaining a precise and full translation from an independent source. Thus, in the late 1970s, several scholarly translations were commissioned. Although the new translations were in some respects better than the original translation of 1969, they betrayed the limitations of the merely academic and scholarly approach. The translators clearly did not understand Swami Muktananda's Spiritual purpose and point of view, and, therefore, their translations did not adequately represent Swami Muktananda's intended meaning in the letter.

Finally, in 1984, an Indologist and scholar of various Hindu Adepts, with a sensitivity to Spiritual terminologies, meanings, and issues, brought to light elements of the letter that had never been translated. The language of the 1984 translation was more sophisticated than earlier versions. Its flowing ease seemed more fitting to Swami Muktananda than the halting style of the original translation, for although Swami Muktananda was not a highly educated man, his language carried a forcefulness and power that had not appeared in earlier translations.

Most revealing, however, was the 1984 translator's discovery of specific language, in the original text of the letter, indicating Swami Muktananda's evaluation of Bhagavan Adi Da's Spiritual development. According to this new version, Swami Muktananda forthrightly proclaims his disciple's Realization by stating that Dhyanananda was Yogically Self-Realized, having "fulfilled the sadhana of dhyana", having become "realized in dhyana", and having "realized the mystical tradition of Vedanta". This new translation appeared to rescue the lost essence of the letter from the original translators' apparent efforts to obscure the Swami's gift of acknowledgement to Bhagavan Adi Da.

Having presumed that a final translation had at last been achieved, Bhagavan Adi Da proceeded in 1986 to write the first version of "The Order of My Free Names", which was published later that year. There the matter would surely have come to rest, had not Bhagavan Adi Da Himself, soon after that publication, raised new questions about several words in the 1984 translation. At His request, the original letter and the 1984 translation were submitted to further scrutiny by new translators.

Bhagavan Adi Da had noted that Swami Muktananda's handwriting becomes both more informal and more difficult to read in the second half of the letter. The new translators discovered that several words in this section of the letter had indeed been misread, and thus mistranslated, by all previous translators. This led them to conclude that the 1984 translator had overstated Swami Muktananda's language regarding the fullness and extent of Bhagavan Adi Da's Yogic Realization.

This criticism of the 1984 translation is more naturally in accord with Swami Muktananda's own position regarding the nature of Yogic Realization and his likely understanding of his young devotee's experience at that time. Swami Muktananda regarded the stable visualization of the "blue pearl" to be the primary evidence of supreme Realization.* However, at the time Swami Muktananda's letter was written (soon after Adi Da's arrival for His second visit to the Swami), Adi Da had not yet experienced the myriad Spiritual phenomena (including visualization of the "blue pearl") that came to characterize this visit. Thus, at the time Swami Muktananda wrote the letter, the only report of meditative experience that he had received from Bhagavan Adi Da was the letter Adi Da had written in 1968 (after His return to the United States) describing His experience of fifth stage conditional Nirvikalpa Samadhi toward the end of His first visit to Swami Muktananda. Given Swami Muktananda's valuing of savikalpa samadhi above fifth stage conditional Nirvikalpa Samadhi, Swami Muktananda would not have interpreted Bhagavan Adi Da's Realization of the latter (or His experience of the internal revelation of the meditative process on the morning of the letter writing) as the supreme Yogic Realization.

Therefore, in 1989, with Swami Muktananda's letter scheduled for republication as part of a revised form of "The Order of My Free Names", a definitive translation was again sought. After all this time, the problems of translation had not finally been fully solved.

---

* Adi Da, in His uniquely complete accounting for all possible forms of samadhi [see *The Dawn Horse Testament Of Adi Da* or *The (Shorter) "Testament Of Secrets" Of Adi Da*] has Revealed that, because it is a type of "savikalpa samadhi" (or samadhi that includes one or another form of blissful psycho-physical awareness), the "blue pearl" is a Realization that occurs in the context of the advanced fourth stage of life and the fifth stage of life. Therefore, the "blue pearl" is, in fact, a potential samadhi in the advancing Spiritual process, rather than most ultimate Divine Self-Realization. Indeed, savikalpa samadhi is not even the highest Realization possible in the context of the fifth stage of life (which is the context of the traditions of Yoga). That highest fifth stage Realization is fifth stage conditional Nirvikalpa Samadhi.

Although Swami Muktananda's letter was written primarily in Hindi, it was interspersed with Sanskrit Spiritual terms. Further, there are a number of places in the letter where he does not follow traditional grammatical rules. Therefore, a definitive translation would require someone who was familiar with Swami Muktananda's own style of writing (particularly his handwriting), yet who was free of the prejudice that had compromised the original version.

An individual with these unique qualifications was located by Adi Da's devotees. A former translator for Swami Muktananda who had lived with the Swami for many years, he not only read Swami Muktananda's handwriting with ease, but was also familiar with his use of words and methods of expression. Thus, in mid-1989, both a definitive transliteration and a word-for-word English translation of Swami Muktananda's letter were finally obtained. Also, because of his unique familiarity with Swami Muktananda, the new translator was able to solve in short order the mysterious salutation to "N" in the letter's opening line. Upon seeing the letter and hearing the question, he instantly said, "Well—this is how Swami Muktananda, not knowing how to spell 'Franklin', would have written it."

With a reliable rendition of the precise words used by Swami Muktananda in his letter of acknowledgement in hand, the final task of revealing its full intended meaning remained. Thus, Adi Da Himself worked on the translation of the letter to reveal the implications and logic inherent within the document itself. Although not fluent in either Hindi or Sanskrit, Adi Da took on this task of "translation", in order that this key incident in His Spiritual Sadhana—Swami Muktananda's acknowledgement of His Realization and Right to Teach—could be rightly understood by all. Bhagavan Adi Da based His work primarily on the original translation by Swami Muktananda's devotees, and the 1989 translation by Swami Muktananda's former translator. In the process, Adi Da Gave Instruction in the principles for translating Spiritual literature and explained how He applied these principles to the particular instance of translating Swami Muktananda's letter.

Bhagavan Adi Da pointed out that everything in Swami Muktananda's letter has significant meaning and that none of his words are redundant. And He went on to show that only through sensitivity to the relationships between words and concepts could the overly literal, mechanical, and reductive quality of the previous translations (including the two from which Adi Da was working) be overcome. He therefore set about restoring (or unsuppressing) the force of logic and interconnection evident in Swami Muktananda's own writing in order to produce the translation given in this book. He describes the process here:

BHAGAVAN ADI DA: The relationship between words and sentences must be taken fully into account, and must be allowed to build up into a structure of meaning. Therefore, the text calls for an elaborate translation. Not to translate it this way is to suppress the voice of the text itself.

Thus, I have elaborated the meaning through multiple words and other literary means to get at what Baba Muktananda's intention was and to make the letter speak clearly. One of the proofs of a proper translation is that it speaks clearly. My translation corresponds to Baba Muktananda's intention, and is not clouded over by the interpretations of people who want to suppress or diminish what Baba Muktananda said, or otherwise use exaggerations of language that make Baba Muktananda say something that he would not say. So unless there is some real evidence for an alternative translation of any of the parts of this letter, I am satisfied that it clearly represents Baba Muktananda's meaning and intention. [Spoken Communications, July 1 and 4, 1989]

Adi Da thus re-created, in English, both the flow of meaning connecting the individual words of the letter and the obvious purpose of each of the letter's sections. Wherever necessary, He also conveys the full range of meaning (both denotative and connotative) of individual Hindi or Sanskrit words or phrases by giving a primary translation followed (in parentheses) by one or more alternative translations of the same word or phrase. Thus, the English text necessarily became significantly longer than the original.

For example, in the last paragraph of his letter, Swami Muktananda speaks of Kundalini and meditation. The original translation reads: "The Kundalini Yoga can be imparted to anyone since the Kundalini power exists in everyone and everything exists in Kundalini." This translation can readily give rise to misconceptions. From reading it, it is possible to suppose that Swami Muktananda was indicating that because the Kundalini Shakti is a universal phenomenon and therefore exists in everyone, virtually anyone can practice Kundalini Yoga. A proper amplification would add that the Kundalini Shakti exists in everyone only <u>latently</u>. While the word "latently" conveys a shade of meaning that is not explicitly stated in Swami Muktananda's letter, it is implicit in the text, and it is clearly in accord with Swami Muktananda's own experience and instruction that the authentic and fruitful practice of Kundalini Yoga requires Spiritual initiation from a Teacher in whom the Kundalini Force has been activated. Thus, Bhagavan Adi Da inserted the word "latently" to clarify the original meaning of the text.

Adi Da's translation of Swami Muktananda's letter given in "The Order of My Free Names" is an example of how it is only such an amplified translation that can be perfectly faithful to the original, by fully illuminating all the meanings and interconnections implicit in the original document.

Transliteration and Word-for-Word Translation of the Letter of Acknowledgement Written by Swami Muktananda in Bombay, in 1969

Transliteration

Śrī Gurudev

priya N, saprem ātmā smaran

1 āp dhyānā me samadhān pāyā hai. aur dhyānā ke sādhanā bhī kī hai. āpko dhyānā me prāpt hai. āp dhyānā me pūrna rūchī mānlīyā hai. dhyāna āpke apne ishtā hone se tume dhyānānanda aise nāmābhidānā kī hai. apko yogamārga me dhyānānanda aise pukār jāyegā.

2 āp Gurudev Āshrām ke eka sachī śraddhālu siddha viddyārthī hai. āpme siddhayoga pradā kundalinī śakti kārya kartī hai.

3 āpne Vedānta bhī jānatā hai. Vedānta ke rahasyā dharma ke mūla mānavatā ke prāptā antar ātmā śakti kriyāśīla hai.

4 jisne dekha ve batā saktā. is (nyāyā ke) uktī ke anusāra āp parāmparā ke niyāmān sārā dūsare se dhyānā karā saktā hai.

5 āp jāhān taka Guru nishtā parameshvara pratī ekātmatā dhyān mānavā pratī samatā aur sanmān yuktā hai. to āpko chītī bhagavatī kundalinī ke pūrna sāhāya dvār. āpko nyāyochita bhogā moksā sampannā banāvegā. iti "śāstra pramānā".

6 āpko āpne kartvvyā pālanā dvārā parameśvarī ko dhyānā dvārā pūjakara paramātmā me ekīkaranā ki tanmayata prāpta ho. iti ashiravada.

7 ye kundalinī yoga sabhi me hone se sabhi ke hone se sabhi me kundalinī rahane se. āp sabhi ko dhyānā kara sakate. dhyānā karnā sabhi ke kartavvya hai.

Swami Muktananda, Thana Jila, Maharashtra Rajya, Bharata

Sri Gurudev

prīya N, saprem ātmā smaran

prīya	**N**	**saprem**	**ātmā smaran**
dear	Franklin	with love	remember the self

1 āp dhyānā me samadhān pāyā hai.

āp	**dhyānā**	**me**	**samadhān**	**pāyā**	**hai**
you	meditation	in	fulfillment	found	have
			satisfaction		
			peace		

aur dhyānā ke sādhanā bhī kī hai.

aur	**dhyānā**	**sādhanā**	**ke**	**bhī**	**kī**	**hai**
and	meditation	sadhana	of	also	done	have

āpko dhyānā me prāpt hai.

āpko	**dhyānā**	**me**	**prāpt**	**hai**
you	meditation	in	gotten	have
			reached	
			obtained	

āp dhyānā me pūrna rūchī mānlīyā hai.

āp	**dhyānā**	**me**	**pūrna**	**rūchī**	**mānlīyā**	**hai**
you	meditation	in	full	delight	taken	have
				relish	acquired	
				interest		

dhyāna āpke apne ishtā hone se tume

dhyāna	**āpke**	**apne ishtā**	**hone se**	**tume**
meditation	your own	what you	it being so	you
		seek in life;		
		what your life		
		is about; your		
		goal/purpose/God		

dhyānānanda aise nāmābhidānā kī hai.

dhyānānanda	**aise**	**nāmābhidānā**	**kī**	**hai**
dhyanananda	such	name being given	to	have

apko yogamārga me dhyānānanda aise pukār jāyegā.

apko	**yogamārga**	**me**	**dhyānānanda**	**aise pukār jāyegā**
you	the path of yoga	in	dhyanananda	will be known
		on		called

2 āp Gurudev Āshrām ke eka sachī śraddhālu

āp	**Gurudev Āshrām**	**ke**	**eka**	**sachī**	**śraddhālu**
you	Gurudev Ashram	of	one	good	faithful
				true	earnest

siddha viddyārthī hai.

siddha	**viddyārthī**	**hai**
siddha	student;	are
	bearer of the	
	wealth of knowlege	

āpme siddhayoga pradā kundalinī śakti kārya kartī hai.

āpme	siddhayoga	pradā	kundalinī	śakti	kārya	kartī	hai
in you	siddhayoga	giver	kundalini	shakti	does	work	is

3 āpne Vedānta bhī jānatā hai.

āpne	Vedānta	bhī	jānatā	hai
you	Vedanta	also	know	is

Vedānta ke rahasyā dharma ke mūla mānavatā ke prāptā
antar ātmā śakti kriyāśīla hai.

Vedānta	ke	rahasyā	dharma	ke	mūla	mānavatā	ke	prāptā
Vedanta	of	secret	dharma	of	root	humanity	of	goal

antar	ātmā	śakti	kriyāśīla	hai
inner	self	shakti	active dynamic	is

4 jisne dekha ve batā saktā.

jisne	dekha	ve	batā	saktā
he	who has seen	he	tell speak	can

is (nyāyā ke) uktī ke anusāra āp parāmparā ke
niyāmān sārā dūsare se dhyānā karā saktā hai.

is	nyāyā	ke	uktī	ke	anusāra	āp	parāmparā
this	argument logic reason	of	saying	to	according	you	tradition lineage

ke	niyāmān	sārā	dūsare	se	dhyānā	karā
of	rules	essence gist purport	others	by with	meditation	have do

saktā	hai
can are able have the ability	to be

5 āp jāhān taka Guru nishtā parameshvara pratī
ekātmatā dhyān mānavā pratī samatā aur sanmān yuktā hai.

āp	jāhān	taka	Guru	nishtā	parameshvara	pratī
you	as long	as	Guru	faith in	supreme Lord supreme Being	towards

ekātmatā	dhyān	mānavā	pratī	samatā	aur	sanmān
oneness identity	meditation	human	towards	equality	and	respect

yuktā	hai
with	to be

to āpko chītī bhagavatī kundalinī ke pūrna sāhāya dvār.

to	āpko	chītī	bhagavatī	kundalinī	ke	pūrna
then as long as	you	chitti	goddess	kundalini	of	full

sāhāya	dvār
help	with by means of

āpko nyāyochita bhogā mokṣā sampannā banāvegā.

āpko nyāyochita	bhogā	mokṣā	sampannā	banāvegā
you appropriate	pleasure enjoyment worldly prosperity	liberation	full of equipped with	make you

iti "śāstra pramānā".

iti	śāstra	pramānā
thus	sacred scriptures	authority

6 āpko āpne kartvvyā pālanā dvārā parameśvarī ko
dhyānā dvārā pūjakara paramātmā me ekīkaranā ki
tanmayata prāpta ho.

āpko āpne	kartvvyā	pālanā	dvārā	parameśvarī	ko
you your	duty	fulfill carry out	by means of	supreme Lord supreme Being	on

dhyānā	dvārā	pūjakara	paramātmā	me
meditation	means	worshipping	supreme Self	in

ekīkaranā	ki	tanmayata	prāpta ho
identity	of	absorption sameness	obtain

iti ashiravada.

iti	ashiravada
thus	[My] blessing

7 ye kundalinī yoga sabhi me hone se sabhi ke hone se
sabhi me kundalinī rahane se.

ye	kundalinī	yoga	sabhi	me	hone se
this	kundalini	yoga	all	within	it being so

sabhi ke	hone se	sabhi	me	kundalinī	rahane se
belonging to all; all's	it being so	all	within	kundalini	dwelling

āp sabhi ko dhyānā kara sakate.

āp	sabhi ko	dhyānā	kara	sakate
you	to all	meditation	get done	can

dhyānā karnā sabhi ke kartavvya hai.

dhyānā	karnā	sabhi	ke	kartavvya	hai
meditation	doing	all	of	duty	is

Swami Muktananda, Thana Jila, Maharashtra Rajya, Bharata.

Swami Muktananda	Thana Jila	Maharashtra Rajya	Bharata.
Swami Muktananda	Thana District	Maharashtra State	India.

The Seven Stages of Life

A vatara Adi Da has described the developmental potential of the human individual in terms of seven stages of life.

The first three stages of life develop, respectively, the physical, emotional, and mental/volitional functions of the body-mind. The first stage begins at birth and continues for approximately five to seven years; the second stage follows, continuing until approximately the age of twelve to fourteen; and the third stage is optimally complete by the early twenties. In the case of virtually all individuals, however, failed adaptation in the earlier stages of life means that maturity in the third stage of life takes much longer to attain, and it is usually never fulfilled, with the result that the ensuing stages of Spiritual development do not even begin.

In the Way of the Heart, however, growth in the first three stages of life unfolds in the Spiritual Company of Heart-Master Adi Da and is based in the practice of feeling-Contemplation of His bodily (human) Form and in devotion, service, and self-discipline in relation to His bodily (human) Form. By the Grace of this relationship to Avatara Adi Da, the first three (or foundation) stages of life are lived and fulfilled in a self-transcending devotional disposition, or (as He describes it) "in the 'original' or beginner's devotional context of the fourth stage of life".

The fourth stage of life is the transitional stage between the gross, bodily-based point of view of the first three stages of life and the subtle, psychic point of view of the fifth stage of life. The fourth stage of life is the stage of Spiritual devotion, or surrender of separate self, in which the gross functions of the being are submitted to the higher psychic, or subtle, functions of the being, and, through these psychic functions, to the Divine Being, God, Truth, or Reality. In the fourth stage of life, the gross, or bodily-based, personality of the first three stages of life is purified through reception of the Spiritual Force ("Holy Spirit", or "Shakti") of the Divine Reality, Which prepares the being to outgrow the bodily-based point of view.

In the Way of the Heart, as the orientation of the fourth stage of life matures, heart-felt surrender to the bodily (human) Form of Sat-Guru Adi Da deepens by Grace, drawing His devotee into Love-Communion with His All-Pervading Spiritual Presence. Growth in the "basic" context of the fourth stage of life in the Way of the Heart is also characterized by a Baptizing Current of Spirit-Energy that is at first felt to flow down the front of the body from above the head to the bodily base.

The descent of Avatara Adi Da's Spirit-Baptism, or His "Crashing Down", releases obstructions predominantly in the waking, or frontal, personality. This frontal Yoga purifies His devotee and infuses him or her with His Spirit-Power. Sri Avatara Adi Da's devotee is awakened to profound love of and devotional intimacy with Him.

If the transition to the sixth stage of life is not otherwise made at maturity in the "basic" context of the fourth stage of life, the Spirit-Current is felt to turn about at the bodily base and ascend to the brain core, and the fourth stage of life matures to its "advanced" context, which involves the ascent of Avatara Adi Da's Spiritual Blessing and purifies the spinal line of the body-mind.

In the fifth stage of life, attention is concentrated in the subtle, or psychic, levels of awareness in ascent. The Spirit-Current is felt to penetrate the brain core and rise toward the Matrix of Light and Love-Bliss infinitely above the crown of the head, possibly culminating in the temporary experience of fifth stage conditional Nirvikalpa Samadhi, or "formless ecstasy". In the Way of the Heart, most practitioners will not need to practice in the context of the fifth stage of life, but will rather be Awakened, by Bhagavan Adi Da's Grace, from maturity in the fourth stage of life to the Witness-Position of Consciousness.

In the traditional development of the sixth stage of life, attention is inverted upon the essential self and the Perfectly Subjective Position of Consciousness, to the exclusion of conditional phenomena. In the Way of the Heart, however, the deliberate intention to invert attention for the sake of Realizing Transcendental Consciousness does not characterize the sixth stage of life, which instead begins when the Witness-Position of Consciousness spontaneously Awakens and becomes stable.

In the course of the sixth stage of life, the mechanism of attention, which is the root-action of egoity (felt as separation, self-contraction, or the feeling of relatedness), gradually subsides. In the fullest context of the sixth stage of life, the knot of attention dissolves and all sense of relatedness yields to the Blissful and undifferentiated Feeling of Being. The characteristic Samadhi of the sixth stage of life is Jnana Samadhi, the temporary and exclusive Realization of the Transcendental Self, or Consciousness Itself.

The transition from the sixth stage exclusive holding to the Transcendental Self-Position to the seventh stage Realization of Absolute Non-Separateness is the unique Revelation of Avatara Adi Da. Various traditions and individuals previous to Bhagavan Adi Da's Revelation have had sixth stage intuitions or premonitions of the Most Perfect Realization of Non-Separateness, but no one previous to Avatara Adi Da has fully Realized the seventh stage of life. He is the First, Last, and Only Adept-Revealer of the seventh stage of life.

The seventh stage Realization is the Gift of Bhagavan Da to His devotees, Awakened only in the context of the Way of the Heart that He has Revealed and Given. The seventh stage of life begins when His devotee Awakens from the exclusive Realization of Consciousness, by Grace, to Most Perfect and permanent Identification with Consciousness Itself, Bhagavan Da's Very (and Inherently Perfect) State. This is Divine Self-Realization, the perpetual Samadhi of "Open Eyes" (seventh stage Sahaj Samadhi), in which all "things" are Divinely Recognized without "difference" as merely apparent modifications of the One Self-Existing and Self-Radiant Divine Consciousness. In the course of the seventh stage of life, there may be incidents of spontaneous Moksha-Bhava Nirvikalpa Samadhi, in which psycho-physical states and phenomena do not appear to the notice, being Outshined by the "Bright" Radiance of Consciousness Itself. This Samadhi, which is the ultimate Realization of Divine Existence, culminates in Divine Translation, or the permanent Outshining of all apparent conditions in the Inherently Perfect Radiance and Love-Bliss of the Divine Self-Condition.

In the context of practice of the Way of the Heart, the seven stages of life as Revealed by Bhagavan Adi Da are not a version of the traditional "ladder" of Spiritual attainment. These stages and their characteristic signs arise naturally in the course of practice for a devotee in the

Way of the Heart, but the practice itself is oriented to the <u>transcendence</u> of the first six stages of life, in the seventh stage Disposition of Inherently Liberated Happiness, Granted by Grace in the Love-Blissful Spiritual Company of Heart-Master Adi Da.

For a more detailed description of Adi Da's schema of seven stages of life, please see "The Seven Stages of Life" in *The Santosha Avatara Gita, The Hymn Of The True Heart-Master, The Lion Sutra*, or *The Liberator (Eleutherios)*.

ADI DA (THE DA AVATAR)
The Mountain Of Attention, 1995

An Invitation to
the Way of the Heart

I do not simply recommend or turn men and women to Truth. I Am Truth. I Draw men and women to My Self. I Am the Present God Desiring, Loving, and Drawing up My devotees. I have Come to Acquire My devotees. I have Come to be Present with My devotees, to live with them the adventure of life in God, which is Love, and mind in God, which is Faith. I Stand always Present in the Place and Form of God. I accept the qualities of all who turn to Me and dissolve them in God, so that Only God becomes their Condition, Destiny, Intelligence, and Work. I look for My devotees to acknowledge Me and turn to Me in appropriate ways, surrendering to Me perfectly, depending on Me, full of Me always, with only a face of love.

I am waiting for you. I have been waiting for you eternally. Where are you?

AVATARA ADI DA,
1971

Having read this book, you stand at the threshold of the greatest possibility of a human lifetime. You can begin to participate in the Divine Process that Adi Da offers to all, by taking up the Way of the Heart. Nothing else in life can match this opportunity. Nothing can compare with the Grace of a devotional relationship to Adi Da. When you make the great gesture of heart-surrender to Adi Da, He begins to draw you into the profound course of true Awakening to God, Truth, or Reality.

Whatever your present form of interest—whether it is to find out more about Avatara Adi Da and the Way of the Heart, to express your gratitude by supporting His Work financially, or to begin the process of becoming His formal devotee—there is an appropriate form of participation available to you. And any form of participation you adopt will bring you into the stream of Divine Blessing flowing from Avatara Adi Da.

How to Find out More about Adi Da
and the Way of the Heart

■ **Request a free full-color brochure about Adi Da, the Way of the Heart, and the community of Adi Da's devotees.** This brochure describes retreats, introductory events, courses, and seminars in your area. It also contains information about area study groups near you and how to begin your own. Please call our toll-free number (on the facing page) or contact the regional center nearest you (see page 176).

■ **Read more of Adi Da's Wisdom-Teaching.** Two excellent books to continue with are:
The Knee of Listening: The Early-Life Ordeal and the Radical Spiritual Realization of the Divine World-Teacher, Adi Da (The Da Avatar), Adi Da's Spiritual Autobiography

The Method of the Siddhas: Talks on the Spiritual Technique of the Saviors of Mankind, a collection of profound and humorous summary Talks from the early years of Adi Da's Teaching Work

Please also see the booklist on pages 177-90 for ordering information and other titles.

■ **Call or visit a regional center** (see page 176) **and meet devotees of Adi Da,** who will be happy to talk with you, answer your questions, make suggestions about the next step you can take, inform you about local events, and tell you about their own experience of practicing in Adi Da's Spiritual Company.

■ **Call the regional center nearest to you** (see p. 176) **and ask to be put on their mailing list.** Or call the Correspondence Department of the Free Daist Avataric Communion in California toll-free at (800) 524-4941 (within the US) or (707) 928-4936 (if you are outside the US), for further information.

■ **Attend the regular classes, seminars, and special events offered in your area.** Your nearest regional center can inform you of forthcoming events. Courses are also available via correspondence. The free brochure (above) provides more details.

■ **Attend a Free Daist Area Study Group.** Call a regional center to find out about Area Study Groups near you, or to create a new Area Study Group. There are more than 150 Area Study Groups throughout the world. They are an excellent way to find out more about Adi Da and the Way of the Heart. Meeting at least once a month, they include video footage of Adi Da and His devotees, study material, guided meditations, and conversations with devotees and other interested people. Our free brochure (above) also contains details and local information.

■ **If you are on the Internet and are familiar with the World Wide Web, you can also find out more by browsing the "Free Daism" Website at URL: http//www.he.tdl.com/~FDAC.** (This Website is rated by Point Survey as being among the best 5% of all Web sites on the Internet.) If you would like to be added to the "Free Daism" electronic mailing list, send a request to FDAC@wco.com. Or you can send questions or comments to our Correspondence Department at the same e-mail address.

**Call Toll-Free (800) 524-4941 (within the US)
or (707) 928-4936 (outside the US)**

Becoming a Member of
Da Avatara International

If you are moved to enter into an ongoing relationship with Avatara Adi Da and His community of devotees, you are invited to become a member of Da Avatara International. A member of Da Avatara International may participate either as a Friend, providing financial support for Avatara Adi Da's Work; or as a student, preparing to become a practitioner of the Way of the Heart.

Becoming a Friend of Da Avatara International

Becoming a Friend of Da Avatara International represents a desire to support Avatara Adi Da's Work, through annual (or more frequent) financial contributions. These contributions support the further publication and distribution of Adi Da's Teaching, or else go to support specific causes which you designate. Becoming a Friend of Da Avatara International is a concrete way to express your gratitude for Avatara Adi Da and His Work. Financially supporting the Spiritual work of a Realized Being has traditionally been regarded as a highly auspicious gesture, a real form of self-sacrifice that benefits all beings.

Many people from all walks of life and all religious persuasions are Friends. As a Friend, you will be kept in touch with developments in Adi Da's Work through a regular newsletter, and you will have the opportunity to attend Friends' Celebrations and special retreats.

To become a Friend, or to find out about the various levels of Friends' membership, call the Central Correspondence Department or your nearest regional center (see p. 176).

Becoming a Student of Da Avatara International

If you are interested in becoming a practitioner of the Way of the Heart, your first step is to formally engage study of Adi Da's Wisdom-Teaching by becoming a student of Da Avatara International.

Like Friends, Students provide support for Adi Da's Work. Students also participate in courses and seminars that provide a lively education about Adi Da, the Way of the Heart, and human and Spiritual life in His

I am here to receive, and kiss, and embrace everyone, everything—
everything that appears, everything that is.
Avatara Adi Da

Company. Classes take place at a regional center, or through correspondence courses. Consult any regional center for information about the courses and seminars that are currently being offered for students of Da Avatara International.

Becoming a Practitioner of the Way of the Heart

Many people who discover the Way of the Heart do not want to wait a second! As students of Da Avatara International, such individuals immediately sign up for a special course that specifically prepares you for becoming a student-novice practitioner of the Way of the Heart.

When you reach the point of complete clarity in your intention to practice the Way of the Heart, you take a momentous step. You make a vow of commitment—in this life and beyond this life—to Avatara Adi Da as your Beloved Guru and Divine Liberator. This Eternal Vow to the Divine Person is the most profound possible matter—and the most ecstatic. For when you take this vow, in gratitude and love, fully aware of its obligations, Avatara Adi Da accepts eternal responsibility for your Spiritual well-being and ultimate Divine Liberation. His Grace begins to Guide your growth in the Way of the Heart day by day and hour by hour, through your practice of devotional Communion with Him.

Taking the Eternal Vow is a formal confession that the devotional relationship to Avatara Adi Da is the overriding purpose of your life. In this disposition you take up the practice of a student-novice and begin to adapt to the total Way of life Adi Da has Given to His devotees. You are initiated into formal meditation, sacramental worship, and the range of practical life-disciplines.

Increasing opportunities to participate with devotees in their celebrations and devotional occasions are offered to student-novices. Through these forms of contact, you are embraced by Avatara Adi Da's devotional gathering and you enter into a new level of sacred relationship to Him. Student-novice practice lasts a minimum of six months. Thus, if your intention and your application to the process are strong, within a year of your first becoming a student of Da Avatara International you may be established as a full member of the Free Daist Avataric Communion, ready to live always in relationship with the Divine Beloved, Adi Da, in the culture of practice that is His Gift to all His devotees.

For information on how to purchase other literature by or about Adi Da, please see the Booklist, pp. 177-90. For further information about Adi Da, His published Works, and the Way of the Heart that He Offers, write to:

The Da Avatara International Mission
12040 North Seigler Road
Middletown, CA 95461, USA

or call:

Toll-Free within the USA: (800) 524-4941
or: **(707) 928-4936 outside the USA**

You can also contact the regional center of the Free Daist Avataric Communion nearest you:

Western North America
in Northern California (415) 492-0930
in Southwest USA (805) 987-3244
in Northwest USA (206) 527-2751
in Hawaii (808) 822-0216

Eastern North America
in Southeast USA (301) 983-0291
in Eastern Canada (800) 563-4398
in Northeast USA (508) 650-0136

Europe
in The Netherlands and the remainder of continental Europe (04743) 1281
in The United Kingdom or Ireland (01508) 470-574
in Germany (040) 390-4438

South Pacific
in Australia (03) 853-4066
in New Zealand (09) 838-9114
in Fiji 381-466

Please see p. 176 for a complete listing of regional centers including addresses.

ADI DA (THE DA AVATAR)
The Mountain Of Attention, 1995

The Life of a Devotee of Avatara Adi Da

Everything you do as a practitioner of the Way of the Heart is an expression of the heart-response of devotion to Avatara Adi Da. The life of cultivating this response to Him is Ishta-Guru-Bhakti Yoga—or the God-Realizing practice ("Yoga") of devotion ("Bhakti") to the Spiritual Master ("Guru") who is the Chosen Beloved ("Ishta") of your heart.

The great practice of Ishta-Guru-Bhakti Yoga necessarily transforms the whole of your life. Every function, every relationship, every action is moved by the impulse of devotional heart-surrender to Avatara Adi Da. The fundamental disposition of devotion is cultivated through a range of specific disciplines. Some disciplines—meditation, sacramental worship, and study—are specifically contemplative, while others—related to exercise, diet, sexuality, community living, and so on—bring the life of devotion into daily functional activity.

AVATARA ADI DA: In every moment you must turn the situation of your life into Yoga by exercising devotion to Me. There is no moment in any day wherein this is not your Calling. This is what you must do. You must make Yoga out of the moment by using the body, emotion, breath, and attention in self-surrendering devotional Contemplation of Me. All those mechanisms must be turned to Me. That turning makes your life Yoga. Through turning to Me, you "yoke" yourself to Me, and that practice of linking, or binding, or connecting to God is religion. Religion, or Yoga, is the practice of moving out of the separative disposition and state into Oneness with That Which is One, Whole, Absolute, All-Inclusive, and Beyond. [December 2, 1993]

Meditation is a unique and precious event in the daily life of Avatara Adi Da's devotees. It offers the opportunity to relinquish outward, body-based attention and to be alone with Adi Da, allowing yourself to enter more and more into the Sphere of His Divine Transmission.

The practice of sacramental worship, or "puja", in the Way of the Heart is the bodily active counterpart to meditation. It is a form of ecstatic worship of Avatara Adi Da, using a photographic representation of Him and involving devotional chanting and recitations from His Wisdom-Teaching.

You must deal with My Wisdom-Teaching in some form every single day, because a new form of the ego's game appears every single day. You must continually return to My Wisdom-Teaching, confront My Wisdom-Teaching.

Avatara Adi Da

The beginner in Spiritual life must prepare the body-mind by mastering the physical, vital dimension of life before he or she can be ready for truly Spiritual practice. Service is devotion in action, a form of Divine Communion.

Avatara Adi Da Offers practical disciplines to His devotees in the areas of work and money, diet, exercise, and sexuality. These disciplines are based on His own human experience and an immense process of "consideration" that He engaged face to face with His devotees for more than twenty years.

As soon as you assume full membership in the formal gathering of Avatara Adi Da's devotees, you become part of a remarkable sacred community.

left: Devotees meeting to discuss their practice of the Way of the Heart
right: Da Avatara Ashram in Holland

left: Da Avatara Ashram, England
right: Da Avatara Retreat Centre in Australia

The principal admonition in the Great Tradition has alway been "Spend time in good company"—in the Company of the Realizer and the company of those who love the Realizer or who truly practice in the Spiritual Company of the Realizer. This is the most auspicious association. Absorb that Company. Imbibe it. Drink deep of it. Duplicate it. Spiritual community is a mutual communication of Happiness.
Avatara Adi Da

Devotees gather for a Celebration meal at the
Mountain Of Attention Sanctuary in northern California

One of the ways in which Adi Da Communicates His Spiritual Transmission is through sacred places. During the course of His Work He has Empowered three Sanctuaries as His Blessing-Seats. In each of these Sanctuaries—the Mountain Of Attention in northern California, Tumomama in Hawaii, and Adi Da Purnashram (Naitauba) in Fiji—Adi Da has established Himself Spiritually in perpetuity. He has lived and Worked with devotees in all His Sanctuaries, and has created in each one special holy sites and temples. Adi Da Purnashram is His principal Residence, but He may from time to time choose to visit His other Sanctuaries. Devotees who are rightly prepared may go on special retreats at all three Sanctuaries.

top left: the Mountain Of Attention
top right: Tumomama
bottom: Adi Da Purnashram

ADI DA (THE DA AVATAR)
The Mountain Of Attention, 1995

As Adi Da writes in *The Knee of Listening*, His Purpose has always been to find "a new human order that will serve to 'create' a new age of sanity and joy". In the brief period of two decades, and in the midst of this dark and Godless era, Avatara Adi Da has literally established His unique Spiritual culture. He is laying the foundation for an unbroken tradition of Divine Self-Realization arising within a devotional gathering aligned to His fully Enlightened Wisdom, and always receiving and magnifying His Eternal Heart-Transmission. Nothing of the kind has ever before existed.

There are great choices to be made in life, choices that call on the greatest exercise of one's real intelligence and heart-impulse. Every one of us makes critical decisions that determine the course of the rest of our lives—and even our future beyond death. The moment of discovering the Divine Avatar, Adi Da, is the greatest of all possible opportunities. It is pure Grace. How can an ordinary life truly compare to a life of living relationship and heart-intimacy with the greatest God-Man Who has ever appeared—the Divine in Person?

There are many forms of response to Avatara Adi Da—from reading another book to becoming a devotee. Every response is honorable. Every response draws you more closely to His Heart. If you are moved by what you have read in this book, the most important thing you can do is to find the form of response to Him—the form of your relationship with Him—that is right for you now.

REGIONAL CENTERS OF
THE FREE DAIST AVATARIC COMMUNION

CENTRAL CORRESPONDENCE
DEPARTMENT
FDAC
12040 North Seigler Road
Middletown, CA 95461
USA
(707) 928-4936

UNITED STATES

Northern California
FDAC
78 Paul Drive
San Rafael, CA 94903
(415) 492-0930

Northwest USA
FDAC
5600 11th Avenue NE
Seattle, WA 98105
(206) 527-2751

Southwest USA
FDAC
PO Box 1729
Camarillo, CA 93010
(805) 987-3244

Northeast USA
FDAC
30 Pleasant Street
S. Natick, MA 01760
(508) 650-0136
(508) 650-4232

Southeast USA
FDAC
10301 South Glen Road
Potomac, MD 20854
(301) 983-0291

Hawaii
FDAC
105 Kaholalele Road
Kapaa, HI 96746
(808) 822-0216

EASTERN CANADA
FDAC
108 Katimavik Road
Val-des-Monts
Quebec JOX 2RO
Canada
(819) 671-4398
(800) 563-4398

AUSTRALIA
Da Avatara Retreat Centre
PO Box 562
Healesville, Victoria 3777
or 16 Findon Street
Hawthorn, Victoria 3122
Australia
(03) 853-4066

NEW ZEALAND
FDAC
CPO Box 3185
or 12 Seibel Road
Henderson
Auckland 8
New Zealand
(09) 838-9114

THE UNITED KINGDOM
& IRELAND
Da Avatara Ashram
Tasburgh Hall
Lower Tasburgh
Norwich NR15 1NA
England
(01508) 470-574

THE NETHERLANDS
Da Avatara Ashram
Annendaalderweg 10
N-6105 AT Maria Hoop
(04743) 1281 or 1872
or
Da Avatara Centrum
Oosterpark 39
1092 AL Amsterdam
The Netherlands
(020) 665-3133

GERMANY
FDAC
Grosse Brunnenstr. 31-33
22763 Hamburg
Germany
(040) 390-4438

FIJI
The TDL Trust
PO Box 4744
Samabula, Suva
Fiji
381-466

The Sacred Literature of Adi Da (The Da Avatar)

A New Scripture for Mankind

Perhaps at some time or another you have wondered—wistfully—what it would have been like to sit at the feet of some great being, such as Gautama (called the "Buddha"), or Jesus of Nazareth, or some venerable Hindu sage of Vedic times, asking the real religious questions that persist in the heart of every serious person: What is the truth about God? What is the purpose of life? What is the meaning of death? What is the best way to live?

Any one of these books by Avatara Adi Da takes you directly into that ancient circumstance of Grace. But what you will find in their pages surpasses even the greatest discourses of the past. The Divine Instruction of the Da Avatar, Adi Da, is not limited by partial vision. These books represent <u>Complete</u> Wisdom and Truth, an unparalleled Transmission of Divine Grace.

After more than two decades of speaking and writing, in constant dialogue with His devotees, Avatara Adi Da has completed His Wisdom-Teaching. To honor the Completion of this extraordinary Revelation, the Dawn Horse Press is now publishing new standard editions of Avatara Adi Da's core Texts, Which He Offers to all beings forever in Love.

INTRODUCTORY BOOKS

NEW 1995 EDITION

The Knee of Listening

The Early-Life Ordeal and the Radical Spiritual Realization of the Divine World-Teacher

This is the astounding Spiritual Autobiography of Avatara Adi Da, the story of the Incarnation of the Absolute Divine Consciousness into a human body-mind in the modern West. Here He describes in vivid detail His first thirty-one years as "Franklin Jones": His Illumined Birth, His acceptance of the ordeal of life as an ordinary human being, His ragged and unstoppable quest for Divine Self-Realization, His exploits in the farthest reaches of human experience, from "money, food, and sex" to the most esoteric mystical and Trans-cendental phenomena, His Divine Re-Awakening and discovery of the Way of God-Realization for all mankind. Unparalleled, utterly compelling, essential reading.

I was captivated by this Story of the first thirty-one years of Avatara Adi Da's Life, by the incomparable Greatness of the One Who Is both God and Man. His Wisdom outshines every dichotomy, every division, every duali-ty. I have come to respect and honor Him as the most complete Source of Divine Blessing—in my own life and in the world at large. I urge you to open yourself to the life that fills these pages. The opportunity has never been so great.

Bill Gottlieb
Vice-President and Editor-in-Chief,
Rodale Press

$4.95*, popular format

NEW 1995 EDITION

The Method of the Siddhas

Talks on the Spiritual Technique of the Saviors of Mankind

When Avatara Adi Da opened the doors of His first Ashram in Los Angeles on April 25, 1972, He invited anyone who was interested to sit with Him and ask Him questions about Spiritual life.

These Talks are the result of that

* All prices are in US dollars.

first meeting between the Incarnate Divine Being and twentieth-century Westerners. Here Avatara Adi Da discusses in very simple terms all the fundamentals of Spiritual life, especially focusing on Satsang, the devotional relationship with Him as Sat-Guru, and self-understanding, the "radical" insight He was bringing to the human world for the first time. These Talks are profound, humorous, and poignant. An essential introduction to Avatara Adi Da's Wisdom-Teaching.

I first read The Method of the Siddhas *twenty years ago and it changed everything. It presented something new to my awareness: One who understood, who was clearly awake, who had penetrated fear and death, who spoke English (eloquently!), and who was alive and available!*

Ray Lynch
composer, *Deep Breakfast*,
No Blue Thing; and *The Sky of Mind*

$7.95, popular format

Free Daism

The True World-Religion of Divine Enlightenment
An Introduction to the Perfectly Liberating Way of Life Revealed by Adi Da (The Da Avatar)

A comprehensive and engaging introduction to all aspects of the religion of Free Daism, the Liberating Way that Avatara Adi Da has made available for all. Addressed to new readers and written in a highly accessible style, *Free Daism* introduces Avatara Adi Da's Life and Work, the fundamentals of His Wisdom-Teaching, the Guru-devotee relationship in His Blessing Company, the principles and practices of the Way of the Heart, and life in the community of His devotees.

(forthcoming)

The Da Avatar

The Divine Life and "Bright" Revelation of Adi Da (The Da Avatar)

The Da Avatar chronicles and celebrates the Miraculous Leela of Avatara Adi Da's Life, from the profound Spiritual origins of His human Manifestation, through His early-life sacrifice of the knowledge of His Own Divine Identity, His subsequent trial of Divine Re-Awakening, the Love-Ordeal of His Teaching-Work with sympathetic, yet Spiritually unresponsive, devotees, and, finally, the relinquishment of all of that in the Victory and Fullest Revelation of His "Divine Emergence", Whereby He Openly Blesses all beings in and with the Sign of His Own Inherent Fullness, Contentment, and Eternal Freedom.

The Da Avatar will delight and inspire readers with the overwhelming evidence of a Miracle and Spiritual Opportunity of the most profound kind: Avatara Adi Da Is The Expected One, Here and alive Now. And He Invites you to a personal, living, and transformative relationship with Him for the sake of your own Divine Awakening.

(forthcoming)

Ishta

The Way of Devotional Surrender to the Divine Person

When Avatara Adi Da gathered with His devotees in 1993 and 1994 at Adi Da Purnashram (Naitauba), He talked face to face with devotees about the essence of the Way of the Heart: the devotional relationship with Him, or "Ishta-Guru-Bhakti Yoga".

AVATARA ADI DA: The True Realizer is not merely a figure, a symbol, an object, but the Realization Itself, bodily and altogether. The Realizer is the Means, therefore, not only bodily but Spiritually, altogether. Everything to be Realized is there as the Master. Everything that serves Realization is there active as the Master. Those who are wise, those who are truly responsive and who find a worthy Master, simply surrender to That One. They receive everything by Grace.

The Way of life I am talking about is Me. I am That—not symbolically but actively—the Siddhi of Means, fully Alive, fully Conscious, fully Active.

These Talks describe the actual process of Ishta-Guru-Bhakti Yoga—devotion to the Beloved Guru—in detail. Essential reading for anyone interested in the Way of the Heart.

$14.95, quality paperback

The Heart's Shout

The Liberating Wisdom of Avatara Adi Da Essential Talks and Essays by Adi Da (The Da Avatar)

A powerful and illuminating introduction to Avatara Adi Da's Wisdom-Teaching. *The Heart's Shout* includes many classic Talks and Essays, as well as stories from His devotees, and covers such topics as the devotional relationship with Avatara Adi Da; the awakening of self-understanding; the Nature of God; the Great Tradition of religion, Spirituality, and practical wisdom; truly human culture; cooperative community; science and scientific materialism; death and the purpose of life; the secrets of love and sex; the foundations of practice in the Way of the Heart; Avatara Adi Da's "Crazy Wisdom"; and Divine Self-Realization.

(forthcoming)

whatsoever that this is true, no matter who you are, no matter which spiritual tradition you follow. Avatara Adi Da is the God-Man, the ultimate expression of the Truth residing in all religions. Of this I am absolutely certain.

The Reverend Thomas Ahlburn
Senior Minister, First Unitarian
Church, Providence, Rhode Island

$12.95, quality paperback

Divine Distraction

A Guide to the Guru-Devotee Relationship, The Supreme Means of God-Realization, as Fully Revealed for the First Time by the Divine World-Teacher and True Heart-Master, Da Avabhasa (The "Bright")
by James Steinberg

In this wonderful book, a long-time devotee of Avatara Adi Da discusses the joys and challenges, the lore and laws, of the most potent form of Spiritual practice: the love relationship with the God-Man. Along with many illuminating passages from the Wisdom-Teaching of Avatara Adi Da, *Divine Distraction* includes humorous, insightful, and heart-moving stories from His devotees, as well as Teachings and stories from the world's Great Tradition of religion and Spirituality. Essential for anybody who wants to know first-hand about the time-honored liberating relationship between Guru and devotee.

This is a warm, loving, and incredibly moving book about the greatest Spiritual Master ever to walk the earth. Here you will find everything you need to know about life, love, and wisdom. I have no doubt

The Ten Fundamental Questions

What are the questions that if answered truly would Enlighten you? You will find out in this simple but challenging introduction to the great Teaching Arguments of Avatara Adi Da. With disarming simplicity and directness Avatara Adi Da goes right to the heart of our modern perplexities about life and God and points to the Divine Way that dispels all bewilderment, a Way of life that is Happy, Humorous, and Free, right from the beginning. A profoundly Liberating book.

(forthcoming)

The Santosha Avatara Gita

(The Revelation of the Great Means of the Divine Heart-Way of No-Seeking and Non-Separateness)

In 108 verses of incredible beauty and simplicity, *The Santosha Avatara Gita* reveals the very essence of the Way of the Heart—Contemplation of Avatara Adi Da as the Realizer, the Revealer, and the Revelation of the Divinely Awakened Condition.

Therefore, because of My always constant, Giving, Full, and Perfect Blessing Grace, and because of the constant Grace of My Self-Revelation, it is possible for any one to practice the only-by-Me Revealed and Given Way of the Heart, and that practice readily (and more and more constantly) Realizes pleasurable oneness (or inherently Love-Blissful Unity) with whatever and all that presently arises . . .

Avatara Adi Da
The Santosha Avatara Gita, verse 78

This is the birth of fundamental and radical Scripture.

Richard Grossinger
author, *Planet Medicine; The Night Sky;* and *Waiting for the Martian Express*

$24.95, quality paperback

The Dawn Horse Testament Of Adi Da

(The Testament Of Secrets Of The Da Avatar)

This monumental volume is the most comprehensive description of the Spiritual process ever written. It is also the most detailed summary of the Way of the Heart. *The Dawn Horse Testament Of Adi Da* is an astounding, challenging, and breathtaking Window to the Divine Reality.

The Dawn Horse Testament Of Adi Da *is the most ecstatic, most profound, most complete, most radical, most comprehensive single spiritual text* ever to be penned and confessed by the Human-Transcendental Spirit.

Ken Wilber
author, *Up from Eden*, and
A Sociable God

$32.00, quality paperback
8 11/42" x 11" format, 820 pages

The (Shorter) Testament Of Secrets Of Adi Da

(The Heart Of The Dawn Horse Testament Of The Da Avatar)

This volume brings you a magnificent distillation of the larger *Dawn Horse Testament Of Adi Da*. Through these pages Avatara Adi Da reveals the purpose of His Incarnation, the great esoteric secrets of Divine Enlightenment, and the means to dissolve in the Heart of God.

(forthcoming)

The Lion Sutra

(On Perfect Transcendence Of The Primal Act, Which is the ego-"I", the self-Contraction, or attention itself, and All The Illusions Of Separateness, Otherness, Relatedness, and Difference)

The Ultimate Teachings (For All Practitioners Of The Way Of The Heart), and The Perfect Practice Of Feeling-Enquiry (For Formal Renunciates In The Way Of The Heart)

A poetic Exposition of the "Perfect Practice" of the Way of the Heart—the final stages of Transcendental, inherently Spiritual, and Divine Self-Realization. Of all Avatara Adi Da's Works, *The Lion Sutra* is the most concentrated Call and Instruction to Realize the Consciousness that Stands prior to body, mind, individual self, and objective world.

Mine Is the Hermitage of no-attention, Where Even time and space Are Watered To the Nub, and I Am Always Shining There, With a Perfect Word In My Heart.

Come There, My Beloved (every one), Come Listen and Hear and See My Heart, and Prepare To Delight In a Feast of Calms, With the Dawn of "Brightness" On Your face.

Then Listen Deep In My Heart Itself, and Call Me There (By Name), and Hear My Word of Silence There, and See Me Where You Stand.

Therefore, Be Un-born In Me, and Feel Awake In My Free Fire, and, By Most Feeling Contemplation of My Sign, Fulfill the "Brightest" Blessing of My (Forever) Silence Kept.

Avatara Adi Da
The Lion Sutra, verses 97-100

$24.95, quality paperback

The Adi Da Upanishad

The Short Discourses on ego-Renunciation, Divine Self-Realization, and the Illusion of Relatedness

In this sublime collection of Essays, Avatara Adi Da Offers an unsurpassed description of both the precise mechanism of egoic delusion and the nature, process, and ultimate fulfillment of the Sacred Process of Divine Self-Realization in the Way of the Heart.

The Adi Da Upanishad *is a work of great linguistic beauty, as well as a remarkable description of the "before" of self and existence. It is a book about the direct realization of Consciousness, characterized by intellectual precision, but also with a depth of feeling that works away beneath the surface of the words.*

Robert E. Carter
author, *The Nothingness Beyond God*

$32.00, quality paperback
(new edition forthcoming)

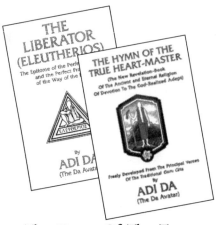

The Hymn Of The True Heart-Master

(The New Revelation-Book Of The Ancient and Eternal Religion Of Devotion To The God-Realized Adept) Freely Developed From The Principal Verses Of The Traditional Guru Gita

This book is Avatara Adi Da's passionate proclamation of the devotional relationship with Him as the supreme means of Enlightenment. In 108 poetic verses, freely developed from the traditional *Guru Gita*, Avatara Adi Da expounds the foundation of the Way of the Heart.

I do feel this Hymn *will be of immense help to aspirants for a divine life. I am thankful that I had an opportunity to read and benefit by it.*

M. P. Pandit
author, *The Upanishads: Gateways of Knowledge*, and *Studies in the Tantras and the Veda*

$24.95, quality paperback

The Liberator (Eleutherios)

The Epitome of the Perfect Wisdom and the Perfect Practice of the Way of the Heart

In compelling, lucid prose, Avatara Adi Da distills the essence of the ultimate processes leading to Divine Self-Realization in the Way of the Heart—the "Perfect Practice", which involves the direct transcendence of all experience via identification with Consciousness Itself, through feeling-Contemplation of His Form, His Presence, and His Infinite State.

Be Consciousness.

Contemplate Consciousness.

Transcend everything in Consciousness.

This is the (Three-Part) "Perfect Practice", the Epitome of the Ultimate Practice and Process of the only-by-Me Revealed and Given Way of the Heart.

Avatara Adi Da
The Liberator (Eleutherios)

$24.95, quality paperback

The Basket of Tolerance

The Perfect Guide to Perfect Understanding of the One and Great Tradition of Mankind

A unique gift to humankind—an overview of the world's traditions of philosophy, religion, Spirituality, and practical Wisdom from the viewpoint of the Divinely Enlightened Adept, Adi Da. *The Basket of Tolerance* includes more than 100 of His Essays on various aspects of the Great Tradition and a comprehensive bibliography (listing more than 3,000 publications) of the world's most significant books, compiled, presented, and extensively annotated by Avatara Adi Da. The summary of Avatara Adi Da's Instruction on the Great Tradition of human Wisdom and the sacred ordeal of Spiritual practice and Realization. A blast of Fresh Air, an immense reorienting force of Divine Criticism and Compassion!

(forthcoming)

184

PRACTICAL BOOKS

Conscious Exercise and the Transcendental Sun

Avatara Adi Da has Given a "radical" approach to physical exercise—to engage all action as devotional Communion with Him. This book explains in detail the practice of "conscious exercise", based on Avatara Adi Da's unique exercise of "conductivity" of natural bodily-experienced energy, as well as "Spirit-conductivity". This greatly enlarged and updated edition includes fully illustrated descriptions of formal exercise routines, supportive exercises for meditation, Instruction on emotions and breathing, and much more.

(forthcoming)

The Eating Gorilla Comes in Peace

When a gorilla is fed, it becomes a peaceful, cooperative animal. When we are awakened to faith, sustained by the Divine, dedicated to the God-Realizing process in the Way of the Heart, we become truly Happy. This book offers Avatara Adi Da's unique Wisdom of the Way of the Heart—the Way that conforms our lives to true Happiness—especially focusing on the areas of diet and health. It offers His Instruction on:

- the most Spiritually auspicious diet for you
- body types and the forms of balancing life practices useful for each type
- an Enlightened understanding of conception, birth, and infancy
- Wisdom about how to die
- true healing
- the ancient practice of the laying on of hands as re-Empowered in the Way of the Heart
- how your diet affects your sexuality
- fasting, herbal remedies, and dietary practices that support your Spiritual practice and purify and regenerate the body as well

(forthcoming)

Love of the Two-Armed Form

What is the most beneficial form of sexual practice for those most intent on the God-Realizing process? How does sexuality become compatible with Spirituality? What is true intimacy? How do we become converted to Love? What is the Yogic form of celibacy and what are its virtues for

185

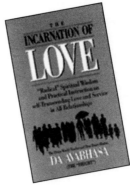

earnest aspirants in the Way of the Heart?

This book is a Treasure—full of Guidance offered by the Divinely Enlightened Master. Avatara Adi Da's own Mastery of the God-Realizing process and of the sexual Yoga that is compatible with that process make Him an utterly unique Authority on the subject. For more than twenty years, He has Worked with His devotees in the emotional-sexual aspects of their practice, bringing His Wisdom to bear in their lives. Now that Wisdom and that Instruction—an essential aspect of the Way of the Heart—are summarized here.

(forthcoming)

Easy Death

Spiritual Discourses and Essays on the Inherent and Ultimate Transcendence of Death and Everything Else

This new edition of Avatara Adi Da's Talks and Essays on death reveals the esoteric secrets of the death process and offers a wealth of practical instruction. Includes such topics as:
• Near-death experiences
• How to prepare for an "easy" death
• How to serve the dying
• Where do we go when we die?

• Our Ultimate Destiny
• The truth about reincarnation
• How to participate consciously in the dying (and living) process

An exciting, stimulating, and thought-provoking book that adds immensely to the literature on the phenomena of life and death. Thank you for this masterpiece.

Elisabeth Kübler-Ross, M.D.
author, *On Death and Dying*

$14.95, quality paperback

The Incarnation of Love

"Radical" Spiritual Wisdom and Practical Instruction on self-Transcending Love and Service in All Relationships

This book collects Avatara Adi Da's Talks and Writings on giving and receiving love. A profound guide to transcending reactivity, releasing guilt, expressing love verbally, forgiving others, living cooperatively, and many other aspects of love and service in all relationships.

$13.95, quality paperback

Polarity Screens

Our bodies may appear solid, but the truth is, we are made of energy, or light. And we appear (and feel!) more or less radiant and harmonious depending on how responsible we are for feeling, breathing, and "conducting" the universal "prana", or life-force. In this book, Avatara Adi Da introduces us to this basic truth of our existence and offers a simple practical method for regularly restoring and enhancing the balance of our personal energy field. The Polarity Screens He recommends may be used with remarkable benefit by anyone at any time. Once you have felt the "magic" of these screens, you will never want to be without them.

It was through Avatara Adi Da's references to Polarity Screens, appearing within His extensive and extraordinary literature, that I first learned of them. Soon, not only myself and family, but also friends, and later also my patients, would try the Polarity Screens and would feel themselves—usually for the first time—as energy. It is the sort of shift in perception that can change one's life!

George Fritz, Ed.D.
psychologist,
specializing in pain control

(forthcoming)

SCIENCE, POLITICS, AND CULTURE

Scientific Proof of the Existence of God Will Soon Be Announced by the White House!

Prophetic Wisdom about the Myths and Idols of mass culture and popular religious cultism, the new priesthood of scientific and political materialism, and the secrets of Enlightenment hidden in the body of Man

This book is prophesy of the most extraordinary and liberating kind. In the teeth of the failures and terrors of the current world-order, Avatara Adi Da offers an entirely new religious and social possibility to humanity. His urgent critique of present-day society is based on a vision of human freedom and true social order that transcends time, place, and culture. He prophesies the emergence of intimate, sacred community, based on Communion with the Divine Adept, the Living Agent of Grace, as the source of healing for all suffering and oppressed human beings.

A powerfully effective "de-hypnotizer" . . . that will not let you rest until you see clearly—and so seeing, choose to act. In modern society's time of troubles, this is a much needed book.

Willis Harman
president, The Institute of Noetic Sciences

$9.95, quality paperback

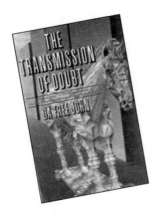

The Transmission of Doubt

Talks and Essays on the Transcendence of Scientific Materialism through "Radical" Understanding

A "radical" alternative to scientific materialism, the ideology of our time. The discourses in this book are a challenge to awaken to <u>all</u> the dimensions of existence in which we are living participants. Avatara Adi Da is Calling us to understand and transcend the materialist dogmas and "objective" stance of conventional scientific philosophy and find the Heart-position of self-trancending love, or non-separateness in relation to all that exists.

The Transmission of Doubt *is the most profound examination of the scientific enterprise from a spiritual point of view that I have ever read.*

Charles T. Tart
author, *Waking Up*
editor, *Altered States of Consciousness*

$9.95, quality paperback

FOR CHILDREN

What, Where, When, How, Why, and <u>Who</u> to Remember To Be Happy

A Simple Explanation of the Way of the Heart (For Children, and Everyone Else)

In this tiny jewel of a book, prepare to find the greatest Wisdom made perfectly comprehensible to anyone. Rejoice in the smile of every page restoring you to your native innocence and certainty of God—and discover the pleasure of reading it to children.

(forthcoming)

The Free Daist

The Free Daist chronicles the Leelas of the Blessing Work of Avatara Adi Da, and describes the practice and process of devotion, self-discipline, self-understanding, service, and meditation in the Way of the Heart. In addition, the magazine reports on the cultural and missionary activities of the Free Daist Avataric Communion and the cooperative community of Avatara Adi Da's devotees. Of special interest is the regular "Hermitage Chronicle", offering current news of Avatara Adi Da's Life and Work.

Subscriptions are $56.00 per year for 4 issues.

For a complete listing of audiotaped and videotaped Discourses by
Avatara Adi Da, as well as books and periodicals,
please send for your free
Dawn Horse Press Catalogue.

Ordering the Books
of Avatara Adi Da

To order books, subscribe to magazines, or to receive your free
Dawn Horse Press Catalogue, send your order to:

THE DAWN HORSE PRESS
12040 North Seigler Road
Middletown, CA 95461
USA

or

Call TOLL FREE (800) 524-4941
Outside the USA call
(707) 928-4936

We accept Visa, MasterCard, personal check, and money order. In the USA, please
add $4.00 for the first book and $1.00 for each additional book. California residents
add 7 ¼ % sales tax. Outside the USA, please add $7.00 for the first book and $3.00
for each additional book. Checks and money orders should be made payable to the
Dawn Horse Press.

An Invitation to Support
the Way of the Heart

Avatara Adi Da's sole purpose is to act as a Source of continuous Divine Grace for everyone, everywhere. In that spirit, He is a Free Renunciate and He owns nothing. Those who have made gestures in support of Avatara Adi Da's Work have found that their generosity is returned in many Blessings that are full of His healing, transforming, and Liberating Grace—and those Blessings flow not only directly to them as the beneficiaries of His Work, but to many others, even all others. At the same time, all tangible gifts of support help secure and nurture Avatara Adi Da's Work in necessary and practical ways, again similarly benefiting the whole world. Because all this is so, supporting His Work is the most auspicious form of financial giving, and we happily extend to you an invitation to serve the Way of the Heart through your financial support.

You may make a financial contribution in support of the Work of Avatara Adi Da at any time. You may also, if you choose, request that your contribution be used for one or more specific purposes of Free Daism. For example, you may be moved to help support and develop Adi Da Purnashram (Naitauba), Avatara Adi Da's Great Sannyasin Hermitage Ashram and Renunciate Retreat Sanctuary in Fiji, and the circumstance provided there for Avatara Adi Da and the other "free renunciates" who practice there (all of whom own nothing).

You may make a contribution for this specific purpose directly to The TDL Trust, the charitable trust that is responsible for Adi Da Purnashram (Naitauba). To do this, make your check payable to The TDL Trust Pty Ltd, which serves as trustee of the trust, and mail it to The TDL Trust at P.O. Box 4744, Samabula, Fiji.

If you would like to make a contribution to Adi Da Purnashram (Naitauba) and you are a United States taxpayer, we recommend that you make your check payable to the Free Daist Avataric Communion, in order to secure a tax deduction under United States tax laws. Please indicate on your check that you would like your contribution to be used in support of Adi Da Purnashram, and mail your check to the Advocacy Department, The Free Daist Avataric Communion, 12040 North Seigler Road, Middletown, California 95461, USA.

You may also request that your contribution, or a part of it, be used for one or more of the other purposes of Free Daism. For example, you may request that your contribution be used to help publish the sacred Literature of Avatara Adi Da, or to support either of the other two

191

Sanctuaries He has Empowered, or to maintain the Sacred Archives that preserve His recorded Talks and Writings, or to publish audio and video recordings of Avatara Adi Da.

If you would like your contribution to benefit one or more of these specific purposes, please mail your check to the Advocacy Department of the Free Daist Avataric Communion at the above address, and indicate how you would like your gift to be used.

If you would like more information about these and other gifting options, or if you would like assistance in describing or making a contribution, please contact the Advocacy Department of the Free Daist Avataric Communion, either by writing to the address shown above or by telephoning (707) 928-4096, or faxing us at (707) 928-4062.

PLANNED GIVING

We also invite you to consider making a planned gift in support of the Work of Avatara Adi Da. Many have found that through planned giving they can make a far more significant gesture of support than they would otherwise be able to make. Many have also found that by making a planned gift they are able to realize substantial tax advantages.

There are numerous ways to make a planned gift, including making a gift in your Will, or in your life insurance, or in a charitable trust.

If you would like to make a gift in your Will in support of Adi Da Purnashram, simply include in your Will the statement "I give The TDL Trust Pty Ltd, as trustee of The TDL Trust, an Australian charitable trust, P.O. Box 4744, Samabula, Fiji, _____ " [inserting in the blank the amount or description of your contribution].

If you would like to make a gift in your Will to benefit other purposes of Free Daism, simply include in your Will the statement "I give the Free Daist Avataric Communion, a California nonprofit corporation, 12040 North Seigler Road, Middletown, California 95461, USA, _____ " [inserting in the blank the amount or description of your contribution]. You may, if you choose, also describe in your Will the specific Free Daist purpose or purposes you would like your gift to support. If you are a United States taxpayer, gifts made in your Will to the Free Daist Avataric Communion will be free of estate taxes and will also reduce any estate taxes payable on the remainder of your estate.

To make a gift in your life insurance, simply name as the beneficiary (or one of the beneficiaries) of your life insurance policy the Free Daist organization of your choice, according to the foregoing descriptions and addresses. If you are a United States taxpayer, you may receive significant tax benefits if you make a contribution to the Free Daist Avataric Communion through your life insurance.

We also invite you to consider establishing or participating in a charitable trust for the benefit of Free Daism. If you are a United States taxpayer, you may find that such a trust will provide you with immediate tax savings and assured income for life, while at the same time enabling you to provide for your family, for your other heirs, and for the Work of Avatara Adi Da as well.

The Advocacy Department of the Free Daist Avataric Communion will be happy to provide you with further information about these and other planned gifting options, and happy to provide you or your attorney with assistance in describing or making a planned gift in support of the Work of Avatara Adi Da.

Further Notes to the Reader

AN INVITATION TO RESPONSIBILITY

The Way of the Heart that Avatara Adi Da has Revealed is an invitation to everyone to assume real responsibility for his or her life. As Avatara Adi Da has Said in *The Dawn Horse Testament Of Adi Da,* "If any one Is Interested In The Realization Of The Heart, Let him or her First Submit (Formally, and By Heart) To Me, and (Thereby) Commence The Ordeal Of self-Observation, self-Understanding, and self-Transcendence." Therefore, participation in the Way of the Heart requires a real struggle with oneself, and not at all a struggle with Avatara Adi Da, or with others.

All who study the Way of the Heart or take up its practice should remember that they are responding to a Call to become responsible for themselves. They should understand that they, not Avatara Adi Da or others, are responsible for any decision they may make or action they take in the course of their lives of study or practice. This has always been true, and it is true whatever the individual's involvement in the Way of the Heart, be it as one who studies Avatara Adi Da's Wisdom-Teaching, or as a Friend of or a participant in Da Avatara International, or as a formally acknowledged member of the Free Daist Avataric Communion.

HONORING AND PROTECTING THE SACRED WORD THROUGH PERPETUAL COPYRIGHT

Since ancient times, practitioners of true religion and Spirituality have valued, above all, time spent in the Company of the Sat-Guru, or one who has, to any degree, Realized God, Truth, or Reality, and who thus Serves the awakening process in others. Such practitioners understand that the Sat-Guru literally Transmits his or her (Realized) State to every one (and every thing) with which he or she comes in contact. Through this Transmission, objects, environments, and rightly prepared individuals with which the Sat-Guru has contact can become Empowered, or Imbued with the Sat-Guru's Transforming Power. It is by this process of Empowerment that things and beings are made truly and literally sacred, and things so sanctified thereafter function as a Source of the Sat-Guru's Blessing for all who understand how to make right and sacred use of them.

Sat-Gurus of any degree of Realization and all that they Empower are, therefore, truly Sacred Treasures, for they help draw the practitioner more quickly into the process of Realization. Cultures of true Wisdom have always understood that such Sacred Treasures are precious (and fragile) Gifts to humanity, and that they should be honored, protected, and reserved for right sacred use. Indeed, the word "sacred" means "set apart", and thus protected,

194

from the secular world. Avatara Adi Da has Conformed His body-mind most Perfectly to the Divine Self, and He is thus the most Potent Source of Blessing-Transmission of God, Truth, or Reality, the ultimate Sat-Guru. He has for many years Empowered, or made sacred, special places and things, and these now Serve as His Divine Agents, or as literal expressions and extensions of His Blessing-Transmission. Among these Empowered Sacred Treasures is His Wisdom-Teaching, which is Full of His Transforming Power. This Blessed and Blessing Wisdom-Teaching has Mantric Force, or the literal Power to Serve God-Realization in those who are Graced to receive it.

Therefore, Avatara Adi Da's Wisdom-Teaching must be perpetually honored and protected, "set apart" from all possible interference and wrong use. The Free Daist Avataric Communion, which is the fellowship of devotees of Avatara Adi Da, is committed to the perpetual preservation and right honoring of the sacred Wisdom-Teaching of the Way of the Heart. But it is also true that in order to fully accomplish this we must find support in the world-society in which we live and from the laws under which we live. Thus, we call for a world-society and for laws that acknowledge the sacred, and that permanently protect It from insensitive, secular interference and wrong use of any kind. We call for, among other things, a system of law that acknowledges that the Wisdom-Teaching of the Way of the Heart, in all Its forms, is, because of Its sacred nature, protected by perpetual copyright.

We invite others who respect the sacred to join with us in this call and in working toward its realization. And, even in the meantime, we claim that all copyrights to the Wisdom-Teaching of Avatara Adi Da and the other sacred Literature and recordings of the Way of the Heart are of perpetual duration.

We make this claim on behalf of The TDL Trust Pty Ltd, which, acting as trustee of The TDL Trust, is the holder of all such copyrights.

AVATARA ADI DA AND THE SACRED TREASURES OF FREE DAISM

Those who Realize God to any degree bring great Blessing and Divine Possibility for the world. Such Realizers Accomplish universal Blessing Work that benefits everything and everyone. They also Work very specifically and intentionally with individuals who approach them as their devotees, and with those places where they reside, and to which they Direct their specific Regard for the sake of perpetual Spiritual Empowerment. This was understood in traditional Spiritual cultures, and those cultures therefore found ways to honor Realizers by providing circumstances for them where they were free to do their Spiritual Work without obstruction or interference.

Those who value Avatara Adi Da's Realization and Service have always endeavored to appropriately honor Him in this traditional way by providing a circumstance where He is completely Free to do His Divine Work. Since 1983, He has resided principally on the island of Naitauba, Fiji, also known as Adi Da

Purnashram. This island has been set aside by Free Daists worldwide as a Place for Avatara Adi Da to do His universal Blessing Work for the sake of everyone, and His specific Work with those who pilgrimage to Purnashram to receive the special Blessing of coming into His physical Company.

Avatara Adi Da is a legal renunciate. He owns nothing and He has no secular or religious institutional function. He Functions only in Freedom. He, and the other members of the Naitauba Order of the Sannyasins of the Da Avatar, the senior renunciate order of Free Daism, are provided for by The TDL Trust, which also provides for Purnashram altogether and ensures the permanent integrity of Avatara Adi Da's Wisdom-Teaching, both in its archival and in its published forms. This Trust, which functions only in Fiji, exists exclusively to provide for these Sacred Treasures of Free Daism.

Outside Fiji, the institution which has developed in response to Avatara Adi Da's Wisdom-Teaching and universal Blessing is known as "The Free Daist Avataric Communion". This is active worldwide in making Avatara Adi Da's Wisdom-Teaching available to all, in offering guidance to all who are moved to respond to His Offering, and in providing for the other Sacred Treasures of Free Daism, including the Mountain Of Attention Sanctuary (in California) and Tumomama Sanctuary (in Hawaii). In addition to the central corporate entity of the Free Daist Avataric Communion, which is based in California, there are numerous regional entities which serve congregations of Avatara Adi Da's devotees in various places throughout the world.

Free Daists worldwide have also established numerous community organizations, through which they provide for many of their common and cooperative community needs, including those relating to housing, food, businesses, medical care, schools, and death and dying. By attending to these and all other ordinary human concerns and affairs via self-transcending cooperation and mutual effort, Avatara Adi Da's devotees constantly free their energy and attention, both personally and collectively, for practice of the Way of the Heart and for service to Avatara Adi Da, to Purnashram, to the other Sacred Treasures of Free Daism, and to the Free Daist Avataric Communion.

All of the organizations that have evolved in response to Avatara Adi Da and His Offering are legally separate from one another, and each has its own purpose and function. Avatara Adi Da neither directs, nor bears responsibility for, the activities of these organizations. Again, He Functions only in Freedom. These organizations represent the collective intention of Free Daists worldwide not only to provide for the Sacred Treasures of Free Daism, but also to make Avatara Adi Da's Offering of the Way of the Heart universally available to all.

INDEX

For information about forms of involvement
in the Way of the Heart Revealed by
Adi Da (The Da Avatar),
see "An Invitation to the Way of the Heart"
on pages 161-75, or see page 176 for details
on how to contact the regional center of the
Free Daist Avataric Communion
nearest you.